PORSCHE

PORSCHE

POWER, PERFORMANCE, AND PERFECTION

SUSANN MILLER

MetroBooks

MetroBooks

An Imprint of Friedman/Fairfax Publishers

© 1992, 1996 by Michael Friedman Publishing Group, Inc.

Library of Congress Cataloging-in-Publication data

Miller, Susann C.
    Porsche : power, performance, and perfection / Susann Miller.
        p. cm.
    Includes bibliographical references and index.
    ISBN 1-56799-391-5
    1. Porsche automobile.   I. Title
TL215.P75M55   1996
    629.222'2--dc20
                                                    96-32633
                                                    CIP

Editor: Dana Rosen
Art Direction: Devorah Levinrad
Designer: Kevin Ullrich
Photography Editor: Ede Rothaus

Typeset by Classic Type, Inc.
Color separations by United South Sea Graphic Art Co., Ltd.
Printed in China by Leefung-Asco Printers Ltd.

For bulk purchases and special sales, please contact:
Friedman/Fairfax Publishers
Attention: Sales Department
15 West 26th Street
New York, NY 10010
212/685-6610 FAX 212/685-1307

Visit the Friedman/Fairfax Website:
http://www.webcom.com/friedman

DEDICATION

To all the men in my life: my father, my son, and my significant other.

ACKNOWLEDGMENTS

The New York offices of the Michael Friedman Publishing Group, Inc. have a fantastic staff who edited my manuscript and researched all the photography. Thank you Dana Rosen and Ede Rothaus.

There are many special thanks that go to my family, whom I neglected when I locked myself up in my computer room. The cat was fed because she jumped on the computer keys when she was hungry. I got fed because my stomach made strange noises. Everyone else had to fend for themselves.

I would like to thank Katrin Müller in the press department of Porsche AG in Germany, who looked through the archives for the early photos of Porsche history. The people at Porsche Cars North America, Inc. in Reno, Nevada, especially Bob Carlson in the racing division and Dan Hopper, deserve a big thank you for their help checking the many early dates and racing wins. Another thank you goes to Ed Triolo, whom I have known for over twelve years, beginning when I started working on my first Porsche book and Porsche magazine. Hal Williams deserves a special mention because he gave me this project in the first place. Many thanks go to Patti Reynolds for her assistance in reading a manuscript about a car she knew nothing about; to Tim Kuser, who taught me how to collect bits and pieces of Porsche collectibles; to Sandy Wagner for her laser printer and crazy jokes that kept us all slightly sane; and to John Kelly, who put up with it all. And last but not least, a thank you to Mom, who knows nothing about cars but who taught me to drive and made me what I am today!

For the 1996 update, special thank yous go to Dr. William (Bill the "Book Man") Block, who kept faxing me corrections each time he reread the copy, and to Tim Kuser, who made the captions so descriptive. I especially want to mention Sylvia Stadelmann from the press department at the Porsche factory in Stuttgart, Germany, for sending me the latest photographs and press material for this new edition. Susan Lauzau, Emilya Naymark, and Kevin Ullrich of the Michael Friedman Publishing Group made it all possible to reprint this updated edition. Thank you all.

CONTENTS

INTRODUCTION

This book is for the world's automobile enthusiasts. It is especially devoted to the Porsche lover, the Porsche "nut" (of which I am one), and the Porsche competitor, both on and off the track.

In any general automotive book found in the library, a bookstore, or even your own collection, the name Ferdinand Porsche will always be found in the index. He is mentioned as one of the greatest automotive engineers of all time, along with Marc Birkigt, Ettore Bugatti, Paul Daimler, Ernest Henri, Henry Leland, Colin Chapman, and Frederick Lanchester, to name but a few. Dr. Porsche designed the Austro-Daimler, the Auto Union Grand Prix

Weissach Development Center.

cars, the Volkswagen, and various German army tanks during World War II. He worked on projects for Wanderer (now part of Audi), Citroën, Alfa-Romeo, Volvo, Fiat, and the list goes on. All this occurred before the first Porsche sports car was built. He also designed airplane engines, fire trucks, and even tractors. Few today are aware to whom we have to be thankful for helping us to go fast, faster, faster!

For the first-time buyer of a Porsche book:
- Did you know that there really is a Porsche family and that they are still very much a part of the Porsche automobile manufacturing company in Stuttgart-Zuffenhausen, Germany?

For both the new and old Porsche lover:
- Did you know that Porsche is pronounced as a two-syllable word: "Por'-sha", not "Porsh"?
- Did you know that the design firm of Porsche (at the Weissach Development Center) in Germany devotes most of its energies to outside contracts? More than 32 percent of Porsche's labor force works on outside research and development for automotive, motorcycle, technological, and aerodynamic corporations all over the world, including the automotive industry in the United States?

So much has been written about Porsche throughout the world that it would be very difficult to develop a book that is all new. But whether you are a first-time Porsche-book buyer/collector or a long-time Porsche enthusiast, this book will be enjoyable and educational. It is a book you will refer to many times and keep in your library forever.

Ten Porsche Milestone Projects Before the 356

1900–1903 Electric Car — The Lohner-Porsche, a gasoline engine generating electricity for front-wheel drive hub motors.

1910 Austro-Daimler — Wins first, second, and third places in Prince Henry Trials.

1914–1918 "Land Train" — Used during World War I to tow heavy artillery on land or rail; gasoline engine generator with hub-mounted motors on each trailer.

1923 Austro-Daimler — Post-World War I, type M, 6-cylinder.

1924–1928 Mercedes-Benz — 2.0-liter, 4-cylinder super-charged Mercedes wins Targa Florio; development of 6-cylinder S models that lead to the famed SSK.

1934–1939 Auto Union — 6.3 liter, V–16 rear engine Grand Prix car exceeded 170 mph (272 kph) (1934), 180 mph (288 kph) (1935); V–12 in 1938. Two world records not broken for twenty years.

1935–1939 Volkswagen — "The People's Car," commissioned by Chancellor Hitler of the Third Reich, a project for an inexpensive, all-purpose vehicle.

1939 Land Speed Record Car — 44-liter, 3,000 bhp Daimler-Benz aero engine, 6-wheel land speed record car designed to travel 400 mph (644 kph); 2.8 tons (2.5 metric tons), 29 feet (8.7 m) long. World War II interrupted final developments.

1940–1944 Tiger Tank — 56 tons (51 metric tons); gasoline-electric power, full armor, and mobile guns.

1942–1945 Maus (mouse) Tank — 189 tons (171 metric tons); largest tank in World War II. Gasoline-electric power; only prototypes were built.

356 Speedster.

IT STARTED AS A DREAM

Page 10: *Ferdinand Porsche stands next to one of his successful designs, the supercharged 2.0-liter Mercedes race car. The photograph was taken at the Targa Florio race in April 1924. The driver, Alfred Neubauer, later gained fame as race-team manager for Mercedes-Benz. Page 11: In 1910, Ferdinand Porsche drove his Austro-Daimler, which he designed, to victory in the Prince Henry Trials in Austria. The three Austro-Daimlers entered took the first three places. Top left: Ferdinand Porsche in 1910, when he was chief engineer at Austro-Daimler in Wiener-Neustadt, Austria. Top right: The Austro-Daimler tractor, powered by Ferdinand Porsche's gasoline-electric drive, was designed to pull the Austrian Army's huge mortar during World War I, making such artillery quickly mobile for the first time.*

Ferdinand Porsche was born on September 3, 1875, in Bohemia (now part of Czechoslovakia) and passed away on January 30, 1951.

EARLY PROJECTS BEFORE THE PORSCHE AUTOMOBILE

From his early childhood, Ferdinand Porsche was interested in experimenting with electricity. In 1895, at the age of nineteen, after working as an apprentice for a year, he became an electrical technician in Vienna, Austria. At this time, motorcars were slowly appearing throughout the world, beginning as a rich man's toy.

In 1898, Porsche joined Lohner and Company, a carriage-making firm turned automobile manufacturer,

and he began designing and building electric-powered cars. At the Universal Exposition in Paris in 1900, the first Lohner-Porsche was exhibited. It was fitted with electric hub motors that drove the front wheels and could reach speeds of close to 25 mph (40 kph), a sure ticket-getter if it could be caught. Porsche was only twenty-five years old, and he already had his name on vehicles being driven on the roads.

By 1901, Porsche realized that to reach higher speeds and to get better performance, he would have to look at the gasoline engine. He conceived of an ingenious design for an automobile that contained both electricity and gasoline. The gasoline engine drove an electric generator that provided electricity for the motors in the wheels. If the gasoline engine broke down, the vehicle could still travel an additional thirty-five miles (56 km) to a safe overnight stop or back home using the electricity in its large storage battery.

In 1906, the Austrian branch of the Daimler Motor Co. offered the position of technical director (chief engineer) to the young Porsche. The biggest seller from the company at the time was a car called Mercedes, and within a short time its greatest competition, on both sides of the Atlantic, was a car from a company called Benz. Porsche

The Beginning of a Legend

The Porsche crest as we know it today was not designed until 1952. The early cars had only the Porsche lettering. The crest incorporates the Stuttgart coat of arms, showing a rampant black horse on a yellow background (the old area of Stuttgart had been a horse stud farm). The black and red colors with the six curved staghorns represent the crest of the state of Baden-Württemberg, and the Porsche name runs across the top.

Above: *Ferdinand Porsche at the wheel of a gasoline-electric Lohner-Porsche at the Exelberg Hill Climb in 1902, where the car set a new record. His employer, Ludwig Lohner, sits next to him.*

continued to work on gasoline-electric cars, and in 1909 he developed his first aviation engine.

At this time, racing was becoming very important to the car-manufacturing communities. By 1910, Porsche devoted himself to winning the Prince Henry Trials for Austro-Daimler by using new streamlined designs for the exterior and an 86-bhp, 4-cylinder engine. The three cars Austro-Daimler entered won first, second, and third place, with Porsche driving the winning car. Between 1911 and 1914, two hundred of this winning model were sold.

During 1917, Porsche was awarded the title of Dr. Ing. honoris causa by the Vienna Technical Institute. Later, he would receive another honorary doctorate, in 1924, and the honorary title of professor, in 1940, both from the Technical University of Stuttgart.

During World War I, Porsche worked on designs for heavy transport vehicles to move military equipment on land and/or rail. His original hub-motor drive was used on flatbed trailers, with the wheels powered by individual hub motors. As many as ten trailers were attached and moved like a train, with a converted gasoline tractor as the engine generator.

At the 1922 Targa Florio, Alfred Neubauer sits behind the wheel of the new Austro-Daimler Sascha race car. The car's designer, Ferdinand Porsche, stands behind the "6." Two such cars swept the 1,100cc class. Unfortunately for Dr. Porsche, the company was not interested in such small cars, and he decided to leave.

From Number 7 to 968

It was decided early on that each project in the Porsche design offices would be assigned a job number in sequence. The job numbers would later become the model numbers of Porsche automobiles. The numbering started in 1930 with design number 7, the Wanderer car chassis. The engineers wanted the contracting company to think that the new Porsche company had past experience in design, hence the number 7 instead of 1. The Auto Union Grand Prix car was number 22. The Daimler-Benz land speed record car was number 80. The 11-horsepower diesel tractor was number 323.

From the first 7 through the latest 968, the numbers continue to increase and get better with age.

As the years passed after the war, Dr. Porsche continued to work for Austro-Daimler, designing and developing new cars for the street. He also designed and built a toy car for his eleven-year-old son, Ferry, which could reach speeds of 30 mph (48 kph) in the backyard.

Porsche continued to develop and design racing machines. During the early part of 1922, he designed the Sascha, a small sports car that competed in the Targa Florio in Sicily. The following year Porsche left the firm in Austria and moved to Daimler in Stuttgart, Germany, beginning development on supercharged cars. By 1924, the supercharged racing car he developed for Daimler won the Targa Florio at a record average speed of over 40 mph (64 kph) over the 67-mile (107-km) course. In 1926, Daimler and Benz merged.

During this period of his life, Porsche was very concerned about the size of the vehicles on the road, and he wanted to develop an economy car for the everyday driver. But Daimler-Benz had no interest in pursuing this idea, or the many other radical ideas that Dr. Porsche came up with, so he moved back to Austria to work for the Steyr group as a chief engineer. He remained there for less than a year before Steyr started having financial problems. So in 1930, Dr. Porsche made one of the biggest decisions of his career: he decided to open his own independent design and engineering office. He moved his family back to Stuttgart, Germany, the automotive design center of Europe, taking some of his associates with him. The following year, the Porsche Konstruktionbüro für Motoren-Fahrzeug-Luftfahrzeug Und Wasserfahrzeugbau became a fully registered company specializing in engines, automobiles, aircraft, and ships. Dr. Porsche's son, Ferry, joined his father's firm at the age of twenty-one, after having studied as an apprentice with both Bosch and Steyr.

One of the first designs from the new company was a 2.0-liter car for the firm Wanderer. After 1932, Wanderer became a member of Auto Union AG along with Horch, D.K.W., and Audi. Racing cars were produced and raced under the group name Auto Union, but private cars continued to be marketed by the individual companies.

In 1932, the torsion-bar suspension system was developed. It was first used by Auto Union for racing cars and later used for the Volkswagen, then refitted for the Citroën and Alfa-Romeo, to name but a few. This same year, Porsche designed a 16-cylinder Grand Prix engine, which showed up later in the Auto Union race car. These Auto Union cars raced all through Europe from 1934 to 1939, with the first win at the Grand Prix of Germany and the next in Switzerland in 1934. Their first winning car had the engine located behind the driver and had a top speed of 170 mph (272 kph); by 1935 the top speed increased to 180 mph (288 kph). It set world speed

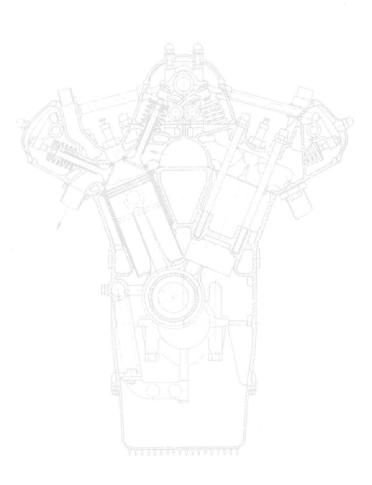

Above: *Erich von Delius driving an Auto Union V-16 Grand Prix car in 1936. The fuel tank was in the center of the vehicle, directly behind the driver, to minimize the effects of weight loss due to fuel usage.* **Near left:** *The right front suspension of an Auto Union Grand Prix car. It was similar to the suspension of the newly developed Volkswagen.* **Far left:** *A cutaway drawing of the 1935 Auto Union V-16 engine. All thirty-two valves were operated from one centrally located camshaft. Dr. Porsche designed this engine to be light, and in a conservative rpm range.*

records that took decades to break, and it was said to be the ugliest thing on four wheels, a hideous monstrosity. But it could win.

Also in the 1930s, Porsche was commissioned by the Third Reich to design the ultimate car for the people, an idea that Hitler had announced at the Berlin Motor Show of 1934, and a project that Porsche had always wanted to work on. The car had to be inexpensive and all-purpose. Porsche and his team built three prototypes in his own garage. The car was ultimately named the Volkswagen.

Right: Ferdinand Porsche at the rear of a very early Volkswagen. Notice the large sliding-cloth sunroof and the radio antenna centrally mounted above the windshield. Below: The cockpit area of the Daimler-Benz T80 land speed record car with all the bodywork removed. The steering wheel is cut off at the bottom to allow room for the driver's legs.

Although Porsche was very involved in the VW project, he continued working on designs for his own company, and he acted as technical chief of Auto Union's racing department until the end of 1937. One project that occupied his time was a monstrous 44-liter V–12 aero engine in a 29-foot (8.8-m) racer for Daimler-Benz, designed to challenge the world land speed record. The car was completed but never run because of the outbreak of World War II. This car, said to be capable of 405 mph (652 kph), can be seen today in the Mercedes-Benz museum in Stuttgart, Germany.

Porsche also found time to design an aerodynamic coupe version of the VW for the Berlin–Rome Rally, managing to complete three cars in 1939. Of the three cars, one has survived and was purchased from the Porsche family by the one-armed race driver, Otto Mathé, in the 1950s when funding for new Porsche projects was needed. This car was displayed at the Laguna Seca, California, historic races in 1982.

Between 1940 and 1944, Professor Porsche contributed to the German war effort by designing a multitude of tanks, including the Leopard, the Tiger, and the Maus (mouse), an impractical 189-ton (171-metric-ton) tank, the largest in World War II. Since the weight of this mammoth vehicle could collapse most bridges and roadways, a special rail car was to be built to transport it, but the war ended before the Maus saw any action.

During the war, the Porsche design and engineering studio moved all the designs, drawings, research, and archives to a converted sawmill in Gmünd, Austria, in order to save as much as possible if Stuttgart was ever bombed. By the end of the war, to keep fully operational, the company repaired farm equipment and war-time Volkswagens.

By 1945, Professor Porsche, his son Ferry, and the professor's son-in-law, Dr. Anton Piëch, were imprisoned by the French. Ferry Porsche was quickly freed, but

Above: The Daimler-Benz T80 land speed record car without its aluminum skin. It was intended to top 400 mph (640 kph) but never ran due to the outbreak of World War II. All four rear wheels are driven. Left: The Daimler-Benz T80 survived the war, but without its engine. The body was made by hand, with protruding side wings added for downforce and stability.

Under the leadership of Ferry Porsche, the son of the firm's founder, the first automobile with the name "Porsche" was built in the summer of 1948. This photograph was taken at the Porsche workshops at Gmünd in Kärnten province, Austria, where the company had been moved from its home in Stuttgart due to the war.

Professor Porsche and Dr. Piëch were not released for almost two years. Under the direction of Professor Porsche's daughter, Louise Piëch, and later his son, Ferry, the company continued to survive.

During the rebuilding of the Porsche firm, they received a commission from an Italian industrialist to develop the Cisitalia (Type 360) for Grand Prix racing. This contract was perhaps the most important commission in Porsche history. The money that was advanced for the design work helped the firm get on its feet financially and supplied the funds used to pay the French government to release Professor Ferdinand Porsche and Anton Piëch. The car was designed by Ferry Porsche and his team for Formula 1 racing; it contained a water-cooled 12-cylinder engine, double overhead camshafts, twin superchargers, and four-wheel drive that could be disengaged at will. The engine was located in the rear behind the driver, and the car possessed a five-speed synchronized gearbox, an amazing feature considering it was built in 1948. The car

was designed to reach 385 horsepower at 10,600 rpm but was never tested. The backer ran out of money before the car ever raced in Formula 1 events (but it did race in later years in Argentina). Eventually, the car was purchased back by the Porsche family and has been fully restored. Today the Cisitalia can be seen at the Porsche museum in Stuttgart, Germany.

After the French were paid the bail needed to release the prisoners (the French later dropped all charges), Professor Porsche returned to Gmünd, Austria, to continue in the pursuit of his dream, to produce a car that would bear his name. This would become the Porsche 356.

By this time Porsche was a very sick man. When he celebrated his seventy-fifth birthday in September 1950, over three hundred Porsches had been produced and delivered to their happy buyers. He suffered a stroke and passed away in early 1951.

But the company was in good hands with his son, Ferry Porsche.

Little-Known Information

In 1952, Porsche was contracted by Studebaker, in South Bend, Indiana, to develop a new car and engine. This project helped Porsche acquire enough money to start construction on a new factory in Zuffenhausen, Germany, a suburb of Stuttgart.

Owning a Part of Porsche

Porsche was a family-owned company until 1972. The members of the family then became stockholders: Ferry Porsche, his sister, Louise Piëch, and their respective children, totaling ten persons, now each held ten percent of the company. A major change occurred in 1984 when one-third of the company's capital stock went on sale on the German stock exchange in the form of non-voting preferred shares. Then one-sixth of the family's privately owned stock was converted into nonvoting preferred shares so that family members could redeem some cash value if they so chose. When the stock was offered for sale, it sold out in three hours—many people wanted to be part of the Porsche legend.

Today, the members of the Porsche family are not directly involved in the management of Porsche AG, but Professor Ferry Porsche, Ferdinand Alexander Porsche, and Dr. Wolfgang Porsche are members of the board of directors.

Porsche Number 1

The first car to bear the Porsche name was a two-passenger, air-cooled, mid-engine 356 sports car. Based on Volkswagen components, it was a hand-built, aluminum-bodied open car, with a tubular space frame, and the engine mounted in front on the rear axle. All later 356s and 911s had the engine mounted behind the rear axle to provide more luggage space and room for an additional passenger. (The mid-engine mounting of that first car was not duplicated until 1953 with the 550 Spyder.) The VW 1.1-liter engine was modified to reach a top speed of over 84 mph (135 kph). It was first displayed to the motor press at the Swiss Grand Prix on July 4, 1948, to great reviews. The company had hoped to be able to produce five hundred cars. The rest is history: from 1948 to 1965 over 76,000 of these cars were produced.

The first Porsche 356/01 can be seen at the Porsche museum in Stuttgart.

Porsche Type 356, Number 1. Handmade in 1948, this car was a mid-engine roadster. The air-cooled, 1,131cc, 40 horsepower engine obtained its cooling air through the two long rows of oval vent openings that ran down either side of the rear deck lid. The "A" at the rear left stands for Austria. The "K" on the license plate stands for the province of Kärnten.

CHAPTER TWO

THE 356
(1948 TO 1965)

The birth of the 356 took place in Gmünd, Austria, in a drafty, decrepit, wooden sawmill. It sounds like the beginning of a religion, and that statement is close to being correct. Porsche collecting today appears to be on the fanatic level, at least among collectors having anything to do with the early automobiles such as the 356, and especially the Speedster.

In 1948, 1949, and early 1950, fewer than sixty hand-made, aluminum-bodied coupes were produced (only four were completed the first year). All the cars produced in Gmünd were hand hammered over a wooden buck, and most of the engine components were manufactured without a machine shop. When you hear "made by hand," that was the truth. Many of the 356 parts, such as the braking system, engine, suspension, and transmission, were taken directly from the VW with special modifications. (This exchange with VW continues even through the 1990s.) Porsches were always designed for speed, as

one can see by the aerodynamic lines even in the early cars. The 356s were nothing like the other cars of that era and were looked upon as being unusual. These early cars were sold in Holland, Sweden, and Switzerland. In fact, it was Swiss backing that made the 356 possible. This was a very difficult time for any manufacturer: Europe was in ruins following the war and metal building materials were almost impossible to obtain.

The Porsche firm moved to Stuttgart, Germany, in 1950 and contracted with the coach-building firm of Reutter to produce the bodies for the new Porsches. The original plan was to have eight to nine bodies delivered a month, but to Porsche's surprise, it received so many advance orders that by the end of 1950, a total of 298 cars had been delivered. (By March 1954, a total of 5,000 Porsches had been produced.)

In late 1951, three engines were offered in the 356. The sales literature at the time touted an air-cooled, horizontally opposed 4-cylinder engine with overhead valves,

Page 20: A restored 1955 Porsche Speedster sitting in front of the former Guggenheim estate, now a park, in Sands Point, New York. Page 21: The seats of a racing GS/GT Speedster. Right: The side view of Porsche No. 1. The body was made entirely by hand at the Porsche workshop on the outskirts of the Austrian town of Gmünd. Most of the mechanical parts were taken directly from the Volkswagen. With its aluminum bodywork, the car weighed barely 1,300 pounds (585 kg).

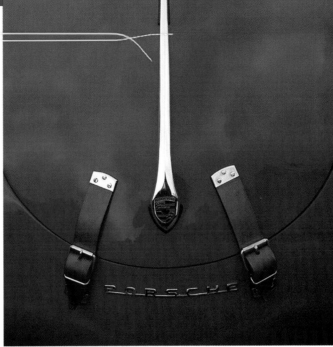

Top left: *The dashboard of Porsche No. 1. The two-piece windshield is supported mostly by the single bar in the center. The instruments have small hoods over them to eliminate glare. The banjo-type steering wheel is very similar to those on the earliest Volkswagens.* Top right: *The front of a Porsche Type 356A. The decorative spear doubles as the trunk handle. The accessory leather straps were used on race cars.* Lower right: *A poster announcing Porsche victories in the 1953 Alpine Trials, where Porsches took four of the first seven places. Notice how the Porsche car is placed between two of Dr. Porsche's other designs: the Volkswagen and the streamlined Auto Union Grand Prix car.*

mounted behind the rear axle. The hot engine for the day was the 1,500cc that had set new world's records at the high-banked track at Montlhery, France. The street car weight was only 1,640 pounds (745 kg), and with a heavy foot, a driver could reach a speed of close to 100 mph (161 kph)—not bad for 1951. As the speeds increased, so did the stopping power. Porsche always wanted to be sure the car could get out of any trouble. When the 1500 Super engine was offered in late 1952, a synchromesh transmission and 280mm brakes were new features. The two models available were the coupe and the convertible.

Racing was very important for Porsche, and awards were very high for its cars on both sides of the Atlantic. Some of the early sales brochures even listed all the racing results for that year.

In North America at this time, safety laws were changing, and any imported car had to meet regulations. One such adjustment was safety bumpers, called over-rider bars, or bows. Bumper guards were added to the Porsche's newly designed bumpers, which had been moved away from the body. The extra bars protected the body from the larger and heavier North American automobiles.

A beautifully restored 356A Speedster with brakes, chrome wheels, and hubcaps from a later 356C. The front bumper trim is a thin aluminum strip with no rubber insert, a stock item on Carreras. The early-style headlight grilles, a factory option, were designed to replace the thick glass covers.

In 1952, Porsche developed, for export only, the America Roadster, a joint idea between Porsche and its East Coast American distributor, Max Hoffman. Designed for U.S. buyers who wanted a car to race, it possessed an aluminum cabriolet body for lightness, and even had a removable windshield. The owner and friend could drive the car to the track, take off the extra weight (even the license plates), race, put everything back on, and return home. Of the sixteen Roadsters that were built, fourteen came to the United States to be sold to Porsche racing enthusiasts.

Porsches were selling all over Europe at this time. A special sales brochure in Swedish was developed for the new and growing market in Sweden. Brochures were printed in 1953, 1956, and 1962 (an eight-page piece on the 356B). Volkswagen Canada Ltd. was marketing the Porsche in Canada and designing its own literature.

The hot sports cars in North America in 1953 were the Austin-Healey 100, the Triumph TR2, and the Corvette. Max Hoffman was having trouble selling Porsches, so he suggested that the factory strip down a car to get it below $3,000, but still keep it comfortable and able to be used for the street. This idea became the birth of the Speedster. The car's basic body was from the cabriolet, with a shortened windshield, a top with no lining, no roll-up windows (just side curtains in case of poor weather), and a bare-minimum interior. Except for the GS/GTs, all Speedsters had a thin chrome strip along the side from the front fender to the back (as did the later Convertible Ds and Roadsters). The Speedster was almost exclusively designed for and marketed in the United States, but the factory printed a price sheet that showed an early attempt to market the car for Germany. The overall look of the car gave it the nickname "bathtub," a nickname that stands to this day. The Speedster weighed 150 pounds (68 kg) lighter than any other Porsche. The car was available in 1954 with a choice of two engines, and the price was perfect: $2,995, but you had to pay extra if you wanted a heater. Today, the car is one of the most sought after models for the street in the 356 line, bringing over $50,000 in many cases.

Top: This 1959 356A Carrera GT displays the optional removable late-style headlight grilles. Bottom: In 1957, Porsche created a special sales folder for its top-of-the-line Carreras named for the Carrera Panamericana (Pan-American Road Race) in Mexico, where Porsches performed extremely well. The Carreras used the famous race-bred 4-cam engine. In street trim, they produced 100 horsepower from 1,500cc.

The assembly line at Porsche, where 1955 cars are being finished. The two convertibles in the foreground are Speedsters, as are the three light-colored cars in the middle of the line. Engine assembly is taking place at the far right.

Also in 1954, Porsches were available with a choice of six different engine sizes: 1100 (dropped in late 1954), 1300, 1300A, 1300S, 1500, and 1500S. Only the two largest models were exported to North America. The 1500 model had no radio, rear folding seats, passenger sun visor, or adjustable passenger seatback. The 1500-Super model possessed all of those features. There were three body styles: coupe, cabriolet (with roll-up windows and padded top), and Speedster. The coupe and cabriolet used the name "Continental" on the side of the car for 1955 in North America only.

Porsche was entering many races and adopted the Italian "Spyder" designation for the 550/1500RS, which it planned to place in limited production as a pure racing car for general sale with delivery late in 1954.

In 1955, the advertising slogans for the cabriolet described the car as the "Dior model of the Porsche family" and "The car women sigh over."

The 356A

The Frankfurt Auto Show, an event held in odd-numbered years, was the place to introduce new models to the public to review in the 1950s, as it still is today. At the Frankfurt Auto Show in September 1955, Porsche introduced the new 356A models for 1956. The changes were very noticeable, including the new all-steel body, still produced by Reutter. The wheel size was decreased from 16 to 15 inches. But the most noticeable change to the exterior was the curved windshield. The interior became truly plush, with a redesigned gas gauge added to the speedometer, oil temperature gauge, and tachometer. A new transmission was also introduced. The 356 Carrera/1500GS was also unveiled at this time, and by 1957 two versions were offered—one intended for competition and the other for maximum comfort and performance.

Wonderful accessories were offered the Porsche customers, including a matching set of fitted luggage for the back seat with special straps to hold everything in place, and even a small bag to fit in the front luggage space behind the spare tire, available in leather or plaid. The most unusual option was a bench seat for the front instead of the two bucket seats. The advertisements read: "A perfect solution to the problem of where to put Junior."

The Convertible D was introduced in the summer of 1958 for the 1959 model year only. Called the "Speedster D" in preproduction publicity, the "D" came from the builder of the body, Drauz of Heilbronn, near Stuttgart. Considered a more comfortable and upgraded car than the Speedster, this convertible had roll-up windows, a higher top with a large rear window, coupe seats, and windshield washers as standard equipment. By the following year, the Speedster was no longer available; only the Convertible D and the luxury open car earlier called the cabriolet were shown in sales literature of the day. It should also be pointed out that the firm of D'Ieteren Freres in Brussels, Belgium, produced the Roadster body for Porsche from early 1961 to early 1962. The firm of Karmann produced a cabriolet with a fixed hardtop ("notchback") from 1961 through 1962.

THE 356B

At the Frankfurt Auto Show in September of 1959, Porsche unveiled the 356B for the 1960 model year with the new T-5 body and a "souped up" Super 90 engine. The bumpers were raised to give the car even more protection.

In 1961, the T-6 body was introduced for the 1962 model year delivery. The front hood was squared off, making it easier to load the trunk. A few added details included an enlarged windshield and rear window for the coupe and cabriolet hardtop. The gas tank was rede-

This page: *Details from a
restored 1955 Type 356
Speedster. The grille along-
side the turn signal (top left)
is to allow the horn to be
heard. The grille on the rear
deck lid (top right) allows
air to cool the engine; there
is no other point of access.
The "Speedster" name
(bottom), plated with 18K
gold, was attached to the
side of each front fender.
Opposite page: First introduced at the end of 1954 for
the 1955 model year, the
Speedster was a lighter-
weight, no-frills Porsche
convertible made to sell in
the American market.*

Bottom left: An Erich Strenger illustration of an early Type 356, used for a sales brochure. Top right: A view through the two grilles in the rear deck lid of a Type 550 Spyder. The spare tire, a requirement during endurance races, was strapped to special saddles atop the transaxle. Bottom right: The bodies of Porsches were manufactured by outside firms through the 1960s. Each company affixed its own badge to the lower right front fenders. This picture shows the badge of D'Ieteren Brothers in Belgium.

signed to allow more room in the luggage compartment, and the fuel filler cap for the gasoline was now in the right front fender with an inside release, so the driver no longer had to open the trunk to fill the tank. All models now had an electric clock, and the double grille on the engine compartment was now standard. (The twin grilles otherwise appeared on America Roadsters, Spyders, and some "A" Carreras.) The two-tone rearview mirror was introduced. With a touch of a button, it cut out the glare of the headlights of vehicles coming from behind at night. Also new was a variable speed windshield-wiper system. The T-6-B stayed in production for only two years, 1962 and 1963, when the new C models became ready for production.

The Carrera 2 was introduced in September 1961, but did not go into production until April 1962. The power plant was a descendant of the Spyder engine—a real quickie, which produced 130 horsepower from its two liters. Available in a coupe and a cabriolet, only one hundred cars were originally planned for production, but the final total was more than 450, some of which were built on the later 356C chassis.

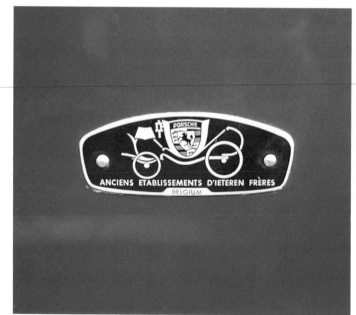

Again, Porsche produced a number of wonderful accessories for the 356, one of which was whitewall tires. Another very rare item was an electric sunroof for the detachable top. The rarest of all, and one that was probably lost forever, was a plastic suitcase for the Roadster that fit over the tunnel hump in the back.

In Thun, Switzerland, the custom coachbuilder Beutler produced a four-passenger coupe. It was truly a four-seater. The rear seats could be folded down separately to give more space, and there was even an area behind the rear seats for luggage. A small number of these cars were produced in 1962 using the 356B chassis; on occasion one will show up at a car show today.

THE 356C

During July 1963, the first 356C model was being introduced for the 1964 model year. One of the major advertising details emphasized the new four-wheel disc brakes, which had been used exclusively on race cars up to then. Three engines were available: the 1600C, the 1600SC, and the Carrera 2. A quote from the U.S. brochure of the time stated: "We spent years developing a great competition car so you can have fun driving to work." Most of the sales brochures were printed in Germany in the language of the country they were to be shipped to, using the same photographs. The accessory

Top: *An excellent restoration of a 1965 Porsche 356C coupe. The SC was offered in 1964 and 1965. At 95 horsepower, it was the most powerful of the pushrod-engine Porsches. Starting in 1964, disc brakes were standard on all Porsches.* Bottom: *The interior of the 1965 356SC. The optional wood-rimmed steering wheel is a much sought-after accessory.*

catalog was usually very detailed, with more than twenty-five pages, so it was not uncommon to see one printed in four languages: German, English, French, and Italian. On occasion, a local dealer produced a one-page handout and saved the more elaborate color brochure for more serious customers.

Production of the 356C officially ended in mid-September 1965. Porsche kept selling the SC in North America through the end of that year, even though the 356C was replaced by the 912 in the European market by April of that same year. Total production of all 356s exceeded 76,000 units.

The 901 was first introduced at the Frankfurt Auto Show in September 1963, but only one prototype car had been built for the show. The new car went into production in late 1964 as a 911; a new era had begun.

Porsche on the Ground and in the Clouds

During the 1950s, the Porsche design studios were involved with new ideas for vehicles used on land, water, and even in the air. Porsche engines were manufactured for a snow tractor, farm tractors with multiple-sized engines (one is on display at the Weissach test center), fire-engine pumps, and even a power-boat engine. The Porsche engine was always known to be reliable, so much so that it could be used in the air: starting in the 1910s, Professor Porsche designed aircraft engines. In the 1950s, Porsche built an airplane engine based on the 356 1.6-liter that could also be mounted vertically for helicopter use. During the early 1960s, Porsche developed and marketed an engine for a small one-man rescue helicopter.

By 1983, work was in progress for the PFM 3200, which was the aviation version of the 911 Carrera engine. One of the major differences between the land-based model and the aero design was that the camshafts were gear-, rather than chain-driven. The flight testing took place in a Cessna 182, and graduated to the Mooney. It was possible to order a Mooney with the Porsche aero engine, which reached 217 horsepower and had the standard twin spark plugs and dual electronic ignition found on all aircraft. A plus for the new Porsche aero engine was the design for the fuel mixture: a single power level, rather than the three controls found on light aircraft, regulated the throttle, fuel/air mixture, and propeller.

The Mooney PFM 3200 was the ultimate Porsche for the high-flying car collector's garage.

Porsche PFM 3200 installed in a Cessna 182 aircraft. Based on the 3.2 liter, 6-cylinder engine used in the 911 Carrera, it made flying easier and more enjoyable through the use of only a single control.

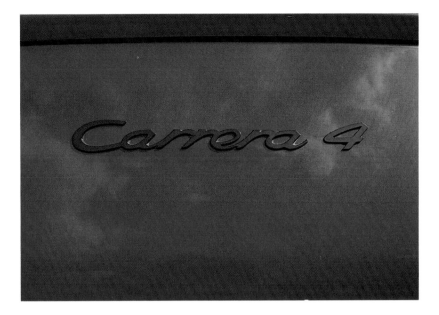

THE 901/911: TRACING THE LONG LIFE HISTORY

The first 901 was seen in 1963. Since then, the body style has seen improvements, but it has always been a little at a time. The car was renamed the 911, the lines have been lowered, the bumpers made larger, and the lights improved for better visibility, but the same basic design of the 1960s is still on the road in the 1990s. Today, the early 911s and 912s are in the price range of both collectors and drivers who want an extra car for fun.

A Porsche is a Porsche and will remain so, but every year the question is always asked: how long will the factory keep on producing the 911? The answer to the question is always the same: as long as there are buyers, Porsche will continue to build it.

911/912

The Porsche factory considered replacing the 356 in the late 1950s. The body style was getting dated, and the 4-cylinder engine was reaching its maximum capacity.

The transition from the 356C to the 911 and 912 took longer than customers anticipated. The first showing of the new body style was at the Frankfurt Auto Show in 1963, but the first cars were not delivered for almost two years. During this waiting period, many changes occurred in the 901, ranging from steering and suspension improvements to small details on the exterior body panels.

By the Paris Auto Show in 1964, Porsche was ready to take orders on the new 901. During this time, Peugeot informed Porsche that it had the French trademark rights to the use of a "0" between two numbers on all production cars. Because the French market was very important to the German car maker, Porsche changed the designation from "901" to "911." However, the first sales brochures published in English, French, German, and Italian had already been shipped to the dealers, so until

the new brochures were reprinted with the 911 designation, the now-rare 901 brochures were given out.

Since Peugeot did not have racing cars, Porsche continued to number its competition cars using the "0," and the numbering system for parts continues to this day to use the 901 to indicate a part for an early 911.

By April of 1965, the 912 had replaced the 356C in Europe. The 912 used a slightly detuned version of the 356SC 4-cylinder engine, allowing greater low-end range and drivability. The price for the 912 was $4,065 in Germany, and $4,690 (American dollars) in North America, while the 911 was $5,475 and $6,490, making the 912 a bargain. This more reasonably priced Porsche was very important, for the higher-priced model might have forced many otherwise loyal 356 Porsche drivers to change to other brands when replacing their 356s.

The first full production year for the 900 series Porsche was 1966. Half of the production was exported to the United States, one quarter was sold in West Germany, and the rest was exported to other parts of the world. A total of 13,000 cars were built, 9,000 of them 912s.

The Targa was introduced to the Porsche lineup at the Frankfurt Auto Show in 1965 for the customer that wanted a convertible-type vehicle. Called by Porsche "the world's first safety convertible" because of the brushed stainless steel roll bar, the Targa featured a vinyl-covered top that folded to fit into the trunk and a soft plastic rear window that zipped out; in 1968 a hard window for the Targa was available as an option for both the 911 and 912 models. Each year new options were available, and by 1966 you could order a sunroof for the coupe. The 911S (Super) was introduced in mid-1966, with a top speed of 140 mph (224 kph); if the engine was driven too fast, a governor engaged to prevent internal damage.

By 1968 the United States and Canada started extensive federal regulations on emissions and safety standards,

and Porsche was forced to make changes in its engines. Thus the 911S was discontinued in North America and would not be reintroduced until 1969.

In addition to the 912 and the standard 911, the 911L (Luxury) was available at a higher price (although the "S" was no longer available in North America, it was sold to the rest of the world). It was the first model year for the 2.0-liter 911T (Touring), which remained Porsche's low-end 911 for six years; it did not come to North America until the 1969 model year.

Also in 1968, the Sportomatic gearbox (not available on the 912 or 911S) was introduced. The option was important to the American market, where standard transmissions were generally not very popular. It was a normal Porsche four-speed transmission, but it was connected to the engine by a torque converter incorporating a regular clutch controlled by two microswitches at the bottom of the shift lever. There was no clutch pedal, but it did require some shifting for high performance. To shift, all

the driver had to do was touch the gearshift knob, thus disconnecting the transmission from the engine and allowing the next gear to be selected. However, the driver or passenger had to be careful not to touch the gearshifter unintentionally or the transmission would be suddenly out of gear.

After the 912 was dropped from the line at the end of its model year in 1969 to make way for the 914s (to fill the price gap below the 911), the only available Porsches were the 911T, the 911E (the mid-priced model), and the 911S. The yearly worldwide production figures were just under 15,000, which also included the last 912s.

The recession hit the car market in the early 1970s. Production figures for Porsche were down to just over 10,000 cars, and a few changes were occurring in the U.S. dealer showrooms. Whereas Volkswagen and Porsche dealers had been operating out of one facility, now new Porsche+Audi dealerships arose and had to operate in separate buildings from Volkswagen.

In 1972, the top Porsche engine size was up to 2.4 liters, more to improve emissions than to increase the power level. The chairman of the board of Porsche AG was Professor Ernst Fuhrmann; he believed that racing was good advertising, and the sales literature of the day projected such. The Porsche factory introduced the Carrera, officially called the "2.7-liter 911 Carrera RS," and made available after modifications to the competition customer as the "RSR." This car was the ultimate fast beast. Built in ultra-lightweight form, it weighed under 2,117 pounds (953 kg) and could reach 155 mph (249 kph) with unbelievable acceleration (0 to 60 mph [96.5 kph] in under six seconds). At 210 horsepower on regular gas, it was the most powerful production car in Germany. As it did not meet North American emission standards for the street, it was sold as a street car only in Europe, but it raced on both sides of the Atlantic. Besides going fast, it looked fast, with its "ducktail" rear spoiler, wide fender flares, and frontal

A 1970 911T. Beginning with the 1969 model year, Porsche lengthened the wheel base by moving the rear wheels back about 2 inches (47 mm), a change which improved the car's balance. Also in 1969, Porsche introduced fuel injection to the 911E and 911S models. In 1970, they enlarged all 911 engines by ten percent (to 2.2 liters).

Top: A 1970 911E Targa. The roof can be removed, folded, and carried in the trunk. Bottom left: The "Targa" name was given to the convertible version of the 911 in honor of Porsche's many victories in the now-discontinued Targa Florio open road race in Sicily. The brushed stainless steel band covers a functional roll bar. Bottom right: The interior of a 1970 911E Targa, showing the air conditioning ducts just under the dashboard and the Leatherette seats.

Cutaway view of the 930 Turbo engine.

air dam for better handling. After many modifications to make it acceptable for highway use, the Carrera was finally introduced to the North American customer for street use (175 horsepower) in 1974.

Again, many new safety changes became mandatory for cars coming to North America. Since half of Porsche's production was coming to the United States, all necessary requirements were readily met, such as reinforcing the doors and adding heavy-duty bumpers to withstand a direct 5-mph (8-kph) impact. The production figures for the cars were again back up to the 15,000 mark by 1973. But in the early part of 1974, when the oil embargo hit, sales of Porsches fell 25 percent in North America and 50 percent in Europe. The Porsche factory went to a three-day workweek.

During this time, Porsche 914s and 924s were being sold along with the 911, and the 928 was being developed. The 911T was dropped, making the standard 911 the least expensive 911 model.

Then came the announcement of the 930 Turbo. Introduced in October of 1974, it was not available to the European market until March 1975, and the North American market had to wait until the 1976 model year. A most exciting Porsche, its turbocharged engine put out 260 horsepower at 5,500 rpm—it was said to be the dawn of a new era.

At the same time, the Carrera underwent a cosmetic change in its tail, from the racing-style "ducktail" to the "whaletail" competition-type spoiler that extended out with a rubber rim around the edge.

If the Porsche factory started to run out of a particular part close to the end of the model year and that part was to be changed for the next year, it was not uncommon to see the following year's updated part on that year's model. This was the case for the Carreras. Some customers received a late 1974 model with upgraded 1975 changes, such as new door handles, already installed.

Silver Anniversary 911S

In 1975, Porsche introduced a special edition, called the Silver Anniversary 911S, in honor of the twenty-fifth anniversary of the Porsche automobile. The car was offered worldwide as a limited edition in both the coupe and the Targa body design. They were all painted diamond-silver metallic with silver and blue-grey tweed fabric interiors. They had an embossed dash plaque on each car with Ferry Porsche's signature, and they were individually numbered starting with the number 2. A number 1 was never produced.

In 1975, the emissions regulations in North America tightened even more. This forced Porsche to change the exhaust system, which decreased the horsepower by 10 in both the 911S and the Carrera. The changes required for the California cars reduced them an additional 5 horsepower. Porsche added new standard equipment and made a few price changes to its lineup for the North American market. With the company hoping to bring in more buyers, the new cars were priced lower than the year before. The plan seemed to work: in 1974, less than half the production was shipped to the United States and by late 1975, 55 percent was shipped.

The 1976 production year finally brought the 930 Turbo, later renamed the 911 Turbo, to North America as a Turbo Carrera, replacing the Carrera there. This car was the quickest, quietest, and fanciest high-performance street car Porsche had ever offered. It was said that the development alone mounted to over two million dollars. The developments Porsche had been perfecting for its racing cars were not wasted, for this was the most controllable turbocharged car of the day. The car was called "a dream car" by the press, and it competed with other exotics from Italy and England. The 930 Turbo had a sweeping rear wing, front spoiler, 7-inch-wide wheels at the front and 8-inch wheels at the rear, with flared fenders, tinted glass, power windows, power and electrically heated mirror, rear window wiper, headlight-washer system, fog lights, leather and plaid interior with velour carpeting, stereo radio with tape player, and air-conditioning. The performance was spectacular, with

A 1975 911 Carrera, with the standard rear spoiler. In the background is a 911 Targa.

The 1976 912E was a limited edition model, introduced to fill the sales gap between the discontinued 914 and the soon-to-be introduced 924. With its lighter engine, the 912E was better balanced than a 911. On the street, the only way to distinguish between the models is by the "912E" emblem on that car's rear deck lid.

The 912E

The 912E developed out of Porsche's need for a car that could fill the gap between the discontinued 914 and the coming introduction of the 924, a car at the lower end of the Porsche market. Only slightly more than 2,000 912Es were produced in 1976 from available parts on hand. It was made with the basic 2.0-liter, 4-cylinder engine (from the discontinued 914) in a 911 body. The 912E was equipped with Bosch L-Jetronic fuel injection (the word for "fuel injection" in German is *Einspritzung*, hence the "E"),

an air pump, and a pair of thermal reactors. The five-speed transmission was standard on this car.

The basic 911 body underwent a few changes to keep the price down. The brake rotors were not vented, and the tire-and-wheel combination was less than the 911. Even the interior was a little less fancy.

Optional equipment included an electric sunroof, limited-slip differential, forged alloy wheels, intermittent windshield wipers, and headlight washers. Also available were electric windows, a remote door mirror, air-conditioning, sports seats, fog lights, and tinted glass.

The owner's manual stated you could go from 0 to 60 mph (96.5 kph) in 13.5 seconds—not bad for a 4-cylinder!

acceleration from 0 to 60 mph (96.5 kph) in 5.7 seconds—an amazing feat for a street car!

By 1977, Great Britain and the United States were producing full-color deluxe editions of the Porsche sales catalogs, with supplemental pieces on the car radio equipment and tires. At this time, the only cars available in North America were the 911S and the 930 Turbo; the rest of the world had the 911, Carrera 3.0, and the Turbo. There was a choice of tires and wheels; if the softer compound was selected with a rating of 130 mph (208 kph), the car had a rev limiter added and the speedometer dial was marked. This option, called the "comfort group," included cruise control (not offered in Europe) and electric windows. The Turbo finally possessed a turbo boost gauge incorporated into the tachometer.

By the following year, the Turbo, with an enlarged engine, and the 911S underwent three price changes as the dollar fluctuated in Europe. This also was the year for the new 911SC, a slightly detuned version of the European Carrera 3.0. It became the most desirable car for the Porsche enthusiast, with rear fender flares to incorporate a wider tire. The Sportomatic was now dropped from the options list.

Meanwhile, the emissions requirements in North America were getting very difficult for the 930 Turbo to meet. Porsche made the decision to stop exporting the car to North America after 1979. During August, when the production year changed to produce the 1980 cars, the Turbos were given the updated changes but were still sold as 1979 cars through December. This was the largest production year for the Turbo: 1,200 cars worldwide, with the last fifty given special numbered dash plaques and certificates stating that those cars were the last U.S. Turbos. However, they continued to be sold outside of North America.

In 1980, small changes that had been offered on the 911SC as options in previous years now became standard, such as the three-spoke, leather-covered steering

A 1977 911S coupe. Beginning with the 1974 models, Porsche restyled its cars to incorporate the new, stronger bumpers mandated by the North American safety regulations. The 911S was Porsche's basic 911 model in North America from 1975 through 1977.

The new 1978 6-cylinder models. The Turbo, in the foreground, underwent a ten-percent increase in engine size to 3.3 liters. The 911C, in the background, had a 3.0-liter, 180-horsepower engine.

wheel, air-conditioning, and electric windows. This same year, a special edition 911SC Weissach Coupe was offered mid-year (see page 83). Only 400 cars were produced, with doric-beige leather interiors and contrasting burgundy piping on the seats, as well as burgundy carpeting with "911SC" burnished into the center. They were only available in two colors: black metallic and platinum metallic. This was also the year that the U.S. federal regulations would not let the speedometers read over 85 mph (137 kph), a decision reversed in 1982.

By 1981, Porsche introduced a berber tweed interior to the 911SC. The 3.0-liter engine continued to produce 172 horsepower, allowing the car to go from 0 to 60 mph (96.5 kph) in less than seven seconds. All the models throughout the world carried the seven-year anticorrosion warranty, which continued from owner to owner. The sunroof option was available, as well as a leather interior and 16-inch forged alloy wheels with low-profile

tires. The right side mirror, electrically adjustable and heated, was an option, and it became standard equipment the following year along with leather front seats, headlight washers, power antenna, and rear speakers. The Targa was priced slightly higher than the coupe.

For the 1982 model year, the Porsche+Audi division of Volkswagen of America and Porsche AG heavily promoted the special program for vacation delivery that was much like the early days of the 356: the customer could order his or her car in North America with all the proper specifications and options and have it delivered to him or her in Europe. After driving around the continent, the customer returned it to the factory to be shipped back home across the Atlantic.

There were standard equipment additions on new cars in 1982 and, with the improved exchange rate, the price increase did not add up to the value of the new equipment, thus showing a net decrease in price in

North America. The major option on the 911SC was the factory-installed 930 Turbo-style rear spoiler seen since 1978.

The year 1983 was the year of the 911SC cabriolet. This was the model that so many Porsche enthusiasts had been waiting for. The first design of the car was displayed on a 930 Turbo at the 1981 Frankfurt Auto Show. Orders were taken more than a year in advance. The first few hundred cars, available only in white or red, were spoken for before they reached the shores of North America. This was the first true convertible offered by the factory since 1965, when the 356C cabriolet went out of production. The new cabriolet was advertised as the world's fastest production convertible. The top had a steel panel between the fabric of the lining and the cloth top to keep the aerodynamically designed roof from puffing up at high speeds, and it featured a zip-out rear window. The engineers were able to retain the same 2+2 seating dimensions, with the same rear fold-up seats slightly shorter than those in the Targa and coupe, whether the top was up or down. The rear seating space was fine for kids, but the leg room was not spacious enough to be comfortable for an adult on any extended trip. Total sales for all models of Porsches for the year, including the 944 and 928, was 21,831. The two major markets were Europe and North America, with the United States receiving half of Porsche's worldwide production each year; half of the U.S. cars entered the California market.

Porsche made changes each year, whether it was a name change, an addition or deletion of a model, or even something as small as a change in paint colors. At the beginning of the 1984 model year, the 911SC was renamed the Carrera, a name reserved for Porsche's top products. The engine was increased from 3.0 to 3.2 liters, and the car could go from 0 to 60 mph (96.5 kph) in 6.2 seconds, with a top speed of 146 mph (234 kph).

The latest special edition from Porsche is the 1993 Porsche 911 RS America. A lighter version of the Carrera 2 by about 180 pounds (81 kg) and devoid of many accessories, it is meant for the serious driver.

The 1993 911 RS America

In 1993 the 911 RS America was introducted. The "RS" designation (German for *Rennsport*, or "Race Sport") was traditionally reserved for the highest-performance Porsches. This version Porsche was designed to handle more like a competition 911. It offered stiffer springs and shock absorbers, larger wheels and tires, and a larger-diameter front stabilizer bar than the normal 911 Carrera 2. It was built in limited quantities for the North American market only, available in four colors: red, black, metallic silver and metallic midnight blue.

To save on weight, the air conditioning systems, power steering, sunroof and rear seats had been eliminated. The armrest/storage compartments were replaced with "RS-style" door panels and simple door pull straps. The sound-deadening materials were also removed from the firewall and rear quarter panels. The retractable rear spoiler, motor and mechanism, was replaced with a large, lightweight fixed tail spoiler.

The RS America was equipped with skid-resistant, black brushed corduroy, form-fitting sports seats, which enabled you to keep in place when accelerating from 0 to 60 mph (96.5 kph) in just 5.4 seconds to a top track speed of 170 mph (272 kph). It was possible to order limited slip-differential, sunroof, air conditioning, and a stereo cassette radio as optional equipment on this model.

The RS America was not for everyone. The Porsche sales brochure stated it all: "The RS never fails to deliver an aggressive, invigorating driving experience where the balance of power and nimble agility puts the driver in control of its unbridled spirit."

The most expensive option on the Carrera was a Turbo Look. The fancy body included the fender flares and the rear deck wing of the European Turbo, and everything else the Turbo had including the high performance brakes—the only thing missing was the turbo engine.

It should be pointed out that driving a rear-weighted configuration vehicle such as the 911 takes a little getting used to. Practice does help, especially if one is in the habit of entering exit ramps a bit too fast. If the driver is not prepared, the car can end up with some of its paint on the guardrail. The weight of the engine causes the car's tail to swing round during cornering if the driver lets up on the accelerator, creating quite an interesting feeling for the driver. Porsche continued to develop lighter exotic alloys to reduce the weight of the engine and transaxle.

The next year began a new era for Porsche. On September 1, 1984, the company's wholly owned subsidiary, Porsche Cars of North America, Inc., took over responsibility for all of the factory's marketing and service operations in the United States. Porsche decided not to renew its marketing agreement with Volkswagen of America, an agreement that had been in force since 1969. The new company would be headquartered in Reno, Nevada, where it is located today. Despite the U.S. change, Canadian dealerships continue to operate as Volkswagen Canada Inc. until December 31, 1994, when all current Canadian Porsche dealers were given the opportunity to enter into franchise agreements with Porsche Cars North America in order to continue selling Porsches.

Few changes were appearing on the 911 models in the mid-1980s besides a revision of the ventilation and heating system. Each year new colors were added and some were taken away. For an extra charge, the customer could always select the "paint to sample" option if the standard colors were not what he or she wanted. By 1986, Porsche started to make products that would have the same performance potential worldwide, made easier by the fact that Europe was instituting unleaded fuel regulations that forced manufacturers to offer catalytic-equipped cars.

After an absence of seven years, the decision was made to export the 911 Turbo, formerly called the 930 Turbo, to North America. The 930 never really left North America, since many individuals had imported the European cars through the "gray market" and then had them federalized, at a cost that far exceeded the new 1986 price. By the following year, the Turbo could be ordered in either a coupe or a convertible, and the Carrera, as always, had both options as well as the Targa as a third choice.

THE 959

It started in 1980, when Porsche announced that it would create a Porsche for the street that could match the performance of a race car. It is hard to determine when the 959 was first shown as a street car. Many of the 911 engineering advances of the 1980s were developments from the 959. In 1983, the 959 was on display as a racing Gruppe (Group) B race car at the Frankfurt Auto Show. The exterior skin was made out of Kevlar and aluminum, and by the following year, the design, incorporating the 911, was copied by after-market shops all over California.

The competition version of the 959 was labeled 961, and a prototype raced at the Paris–Dakar rally (which it won in 1984). Customers were anxious to know when it would be a street car and whether it would be federalized to come to the United States and Canada. But the factory had no comment.

By 1987, this four-wheel-drive, six-speed transmission car was being driven on the roads in Europe. The top

The rear of the fantastic and instantly successful 1983 Group B design study, which became the 959.

speed was said to be over 193 mph (311 kph), accelerating from 0 to 60 mph (96.5 kph) in 3.7 seconds, though there are not too many streets where one can go that fast. Even though the North American market was also very interested in the 959, it was decided that the car could not meet the emissions and bumper-height regulations needed for federalization. It would have been too costly to make these changes for only the limited number that would have been produced for that market.

Anyone who has ever driven a 959 cannot say enough about it; they rave, and they get this far-off look in their eyes, as if they have been somewhere out in the cosmos and have returned to tell about it.

THE 1990S

The full Porsche lineup for 1991 included the 944 coupe and cabriolet (discontinued worldwide for 1992 and replaced by the 968 six-speed [see page 82]), the 928S4 and 928GT, and a total of ten different combinations for the 911 model, including the top-of-the-line 911 Turbo.

Porsche stands for perfection. That sounds just like the company's advertising campaign, but anyone who looks at the new cars each year cannot doubt that these cars are outstanding. In the 1990s, the classic 911 became available in the Carrera 2 and the Carrera 4, the latter with fully automatic, "intelligent" all-wheel drive. Both models have the 6-cylinder engine and 247 horsepower at 6,100 rpm and can accelerate from 0 to 60 mph (96.5 kph) in 5.5 seconds. This 3.6-liter engine continues to be air-cooled with a top speed of 162 mph (261 kph). The only places to add water are the windshield and headlight washer reservoir.

The Carrera 2 and the 4 could be called the ultimate driving machines. The body could be ordered in all three styles: coupe, Targa, and cabriolet. The rear features a spoiler that lays flat on the engine lid but extends auto-

matically as higher speeds are reached for improved handling and additional engine cooling. It also retracts below 10 mph (16 kph). The Porsche owner's manual states that "if the spoiler does not extend at speeds above 80 kph (50 mph), a warning light will appear in the instrument cluster. If the rear spoiler does not extend at high speeds, driving stability will be impaired by the resulting rear axle lift-off." So beware, but if that happens, the rear spoiler can always be extended manually using a lift switch.

In the spring of 1990, the new Tiptronic transmission became available on the Carrera 2. Resembling the Sportomatic of the 1960s, the Tiptronic allowed the driver to shift gears manually without a clutch or use as a full automatic at any time. The acceleration is 0 to 60 mph (96.5 kph) in 6.4 seconds with a top speed of 159 mph (256 kph). The same car with a five-speed transmission could go from 0 to 60 mph (96.5 kph) in 5.5 seconds.

Opposite page: The Group B design was based on the 911 roofline and doors, but everything else was new. Painted mother-of-pearl white, it caught the imagination of car lovers worldwide. Above: The 1991 Porsche 911 Carrera 2 coupe. Although it looks very similar to the 911 made since 1965, it has been extensively reworked underneath.

The next step in ultimate driving was the Carrera 4 (or the 964), featuring the all-wheel-drive system that senses which wheels have the most traction in order to utilize added power and reduce power to wheels that don't need it. In addition, the drive system computer engages the multidisc clutches as needed: one clutch controls the torque dividing the front to rear and overrides the normal torque split of 31 percent front and 69 percent rear. The second clutch serves as an automatic variable-ratio, limited-slip differential between the rear wheels. It gets you where you are going with outstanding performance and produces excellent steering control in curves, with the same engine as the Carrera 2. The Tiptronic was not an option on this all-wheel-drive Porsche.

There were lots of different combinations that increased or decreased the price of the different 911 models depending on the body-style selection. Standard equipment included air bags for both driver and front seat passenger, antilock braking system, partial leather seats, a special race-tuned suspension, air-conditioning with climate control, power-assisted steering, power windows, analog instrumentation on the five-speed, and an on-board trip computer on the Tiptronic models. The list went on, including ZR-rated tires, cruise control, electric sliding sunroof on the coupe and a power-operated top on the cabriolet, an alarm system, heated windshield and heated washer nozzles, and even a digital stereo cassette radio.

The 911 lineup for 1992 included twelve different variations of the coupe, cabriolet, or Targa 911. Featured in this lineup were three Carrera 2 models, the Carrera 4, the limited edition 911 America Roadster (see page 64),

A 1992 911 Carrera 2
cabriolet.

The Turbo

The original idea of turbocharging a 911 goes back as far as the early 1970s with the racing 917 series. By 1973, testing had been completed on the 911 flat-6 motor, when Porsche decided to display a car at the Paris Auto Show the following fall. Externally, the car had fender flares, a front air dam, and a rear spoiler (tray-style) much like the Carrera RS. During this same time, using the same technology, Porsche was developing a full racing version, later called the Carrera RSR, for 1974. This allowed the engineers at the Weissach Development Center the use of a sufficiently strong chassis for testing turbocharging for reliability in actual racing events.

When the new car was announced, its production name became the 930 Turbo. This was the first time a turbocharged system had been used on a standard production Porsche. It was designed to travel in the fast lane at high speeds, but it could also lag along in stop-and-go traffic in all gears without jerking—just smooth, quiet driving. The interior was as plush as Porsche owners expected. The car went from 0 to 60 mph (96.5 kph) in 5.5 seconds with a top speed of 150 mph (241 kph). Said to be too powerful for the average driver, the car could accelerate so quickly that the driver would not realize how quickly until it had gotten beyond the speed limit.

Minor changes were made on the 930 for each model year. The interior appointments on the 930 Turbo were luxurious compared to other models' standard equipment. The owner could select from a wide choice of leather or cloth materials. The major differences between the standard 911 line and the 930 were the suspension and a running gear to handle the turbo power. The brakes were the normal ventilated discs on all four corners, even though the show cars displayed cross-drilled brakes. The shocks

and roll bars were stiffer than those on the 911, and the tires were wider to give the car a more stable ride. The alloy wheels were 7 inches at the front and 8 inches at the rear, and the transmission used was a stronger four-speed instead of the 911 five-speed. In addition, the rear engine lid had the raised words "Turbo Carrera" (in Europe only "Turbo"). In 1976, the rear spoiler was made larger, with two air intakes so that more air could be transferred to the engine and air-conditioner. When the wider wheels and tires were added, the front wheel openings were flared.

The initial North American engine possessed thermal reactors and an air pump to meet the emissions laws. This caused a decrease in the horsepower compared to the European engines—245 vs. 260 horsepower at 5,500 rpm. (By 1979, all turbos had air pumps.) There was a visual difference between a North American 930 and those for all other markets. The North American version did not have the rear fog lamp mounted under the left side bumper extension, the rear reflectors in the rubber bumper strips, or the two small rectangular lights just ahead of the doors (which were directionals only).

In 1977, for the 1978 model year, Porsche increased the car's power to an unbelievable 300 horsepower (265 for North America). The Turbo could now go from 0 to 60 mph (96.5 kph) in 5.3 seconds. The brakes were improved for quicker stopping and now had the cross-ventilated discs with the four-piston calipers from the racing 917, as seen on the 1974 Turbo prototypes. The external difference between the early Turbos and the later models was the redesigned rear spoiler with one intake area with louvers facing forward and a high rubber edge.

The last of the North American 930 Turbos were delivered by the end of the 1979 model year, after emissions laws became too strict for this car to meet the requirements. It was still produced for the European market, and many Porsche enthusiasts purchased the cars through Europe and had them federalized to U.S. and Canadian specifications at a very dear price.

By 1986, the Turbo was back in North America as part of the Porsche lineup. Now called the 911 Turbo, it was available worldwide, meeting every country's regulations.

A new body style was an option for the 911 Turbo in 1987, which had the appearance of the 935 race car. The new look, called the 930S, included a sloping nose with retractable headlights. There were air scoops in front of the rear wheels to help cool the engine and brakes, and small functional air vent slits behind the headlights to allow air to escape from the wheel well, further reducing lift. The body style could also be ordered on the coupe, Targa, or cabriolet.

For the 1990s, a new Turbo was on the drawing boards. For the 1992 model year, more than seventeen years after the earliest turbocharged production car, top track speed was 168 mph (270 kph) with acceleration of 0 to 60 mph (96.5 kph) in 4.8 seconds. The 3.3-liter, 6-cylinder, water-cooled, horizontally opposed turbocharged engine was rated at 315 horsepower at 5,750 rpm. Much was improved, including the new exhaust system, a larger air-to-air intercooler, and an electronic ignition system now fully computerized to minimize emissions and increase power.

In addition, the body was redesigned, with contoured bumpers front and rear and the new aerodynamic front and rear spoiler. The side-view mirrors on each door were also changed in shape. The 17-inch lightweight alloy wheels were now 7 inches wide in front and 9 inches wide at the rear. The underside included suspension changes and upgrades from engineering experience on the race cars. In addition, the five-speed transmission was revised with sportier gear ratios.

There isn't much more to ask for on this 911 Turbo. Standard equipment includes air bags for both the driver and passenger, antilock braking system, ZR-rated steel-belted radial tires, air-conditioning with automatic climate control, and tinted windows. The leather bucket seats recline and have electric height adjustments, and the radio includes an AM/FM digital stereo and cassette with eight speakers. There are also power windows, an electric sunroof, heated windshield-washer nozzles, heated outside mirrors, and an alarm system that shows that it is engaged by a blinking light on the top of the door lock buttons. The only options available are special metallic paint, limited-slip differential, a compact disc player, heated front seats, an electrically controlled lumbar support seat, sports seats, and the gathered-leather seat upholstery.

The next-generation 911 Turbo was produced for the 1994 model year. This revised 3.6-liter engine produced 355 horsepower and accelerated from 0 to 60 mph (96.5 kph) in 4.7 seconds.

The new 1996 Porsche 911 Turbo was inspired by the legendary Porsche 959, acknowledged as one of the great "wish cars" of the twentieth century (see page 53). The 1996 version is the latest generation in the twenty-one-year history of this thoroughbred. This new edition features the same concepts of the 959 in a less expensive production car that meets all the federal regulations and is designed to be driven on the roads in North America. The 3.6-liter, twin-turbocharged engine develops an impressive 400 horsepower and can accelerate from 0 to 60 mph (96.5 kph) in a

remarkable 4.4 seconds with a top track speed of 180 miles per hour (290 kph). There are major differences between the 1994 single-turbo model and the 1996 twin-turbocharged model, which has two intercoolers, knock sensors, three-way catalytic converters with Lambda control, and OBD II (on-board diagnostics, second generation—a federally mandated system for all cars) equipment, and multiport sequential fuel injection. The transmission has been increased from a five-speed to a six-speed; the single-exhaust is now a twin-exhaust; rear-wheel drive is now all-wheel drive; and the early semi-trailing link rear suspension has been upgraded to the new LSA (Lightweight-Stable-Agile) multilink design. The antilock braking system is the new ABS 5 design and the body shell has been made stronger. The changes are not just under the shell: the distinctive fender flares and rear wing have been totally

redesigned to give a 0.34 coefficient of drag. Porsche engineers have developed an aluminum wheel with hollow spokes, reducing the unsprung weight as well as the car's overall weight. The 8-inch-wide, 18-inch-diameter front wheels have "Z" rated 225/40 tires, while the 10-inch rear wheels use 285/30 tires.

The engineers developed a double-cone synchromesh on first and second gears to reduce the shifting effort by 40 percent, along with a clutch that needs 25 percent less effort and 15 percent less travel, making it easier to drive in and around town.

This new 1996 Porsche 911 Turbo is the most powerful production Porsche ever offered for sale on this continent; it accelerated from 0 to 60 (96.5kph) in 4 short seconds. It is a supercar, it is a head turner, it is a rocket!

the 911 RS America (see page 51), the European Carrera RS, two versions of the for-racing-only 911 Carrera Cup car, and the 911 Turbo, available only as a coupe (see page 57). By March 1993, Porsche had a total of nineteen different models to choose from, including the 911 Speedster, the 911 Turbo 3.6, and the Carrera 4 coupe. All these were introduced early as 1994 models.

Since 1993 was the thirtieth anniversary of the 911, a commemorative run of Carrera 4s with the Turbo-look bodyshell was produced. The special features included a full leather interior and special paint, and the 911 stylized badge was underlined with the words "30 Jahre" on the engine lid. The factory produced only 911 cars for this special event. The year 1993 was also noteworthy at Porsche for another important reason: it turned out to be the smallest production year since the start of 911 pro-

duction. In order to gain control of the ever-escalating price of their cars, Porsche had to reduce the number of man-hours it took to build them. The factory started to make changes.

The Speedster was introduced as a 1994 model. It was only built on the Carrera 2 chassis with a special, low windshield and a simplified low-slung top that could be raised and lowered efficiently—in less than a minute the top could be completely hidden away under the composite cover. Porsche called this top "an emergency device." This car was designed to run with the top down. The standard seats were Recaro buckets. Available as an option were electrical height adjustment and the multifunctional Carrera 2 seat with heat for those chilly days when you wanted to drive with the top down and the heat on high. Tiptronic was another option. The door handles were vinyl pulls and were color-coded to the exterior body, as were the gear shift lever, boot around the handbrake, and background around the instrument cluster. The wheels were painted to match the body. Fewer than 1,000 were produced with less than half coming to North America.

1995 AND 1996 MODEL YEAR— MORE CAR, MORE SPEED, MORE FUN FOR LESS MONEY

In order to keep its North American customers interested and coming back for more in 1995, Porsche cut its prices for the new Type 993 Carrera (dropping the "2" from Carrera 2) coupe and cabriolet versions. The official unveiling was at the 1993 Frankfurt Automobile Salon. The body was redesigned, widened by 3 inches from the Carrera 2 model, with flush-mounted glass, lowered fenders, new bumper design (which incorporated air vents for the air conditioning condenser), oil cooler, and the larger disc brakes. The headlights were replaced with the new polyellipsoid low beams and variable focus high beams, changing the front appearance by virtue of their flatter design.

The rear retractable spoiler was now slightly larger and had a reshaped lip, and the taillight glass stretched around the rear of the car. Hydraulic valve lifters were added to cut down on maintenance expense, which also reduced the engine noise and improved the cold start emissions. Even though the engine remained a 3.6-liter, with the new dual exhaust and revised electronics and internal modifications, the horsepower increased from 247 to 270. Its top track speed was 168 mph (270 kph).

The 1996 turbo horsepower has increased from 355 to 400 (see page 102). Now featured on all Porsches, the new six-speed gearbox was developed for this new car, and will get you where you want to go; the new brakes (ABS 5) with cross-drilled rotors really stop you when you get there. Make sure you know if anyone is coming up

The 1996 Carrera Targa (on right) provides more safety features, better visibility, and vastly improved handling over the first Targa, also shown here. Both cars were unveiled to the public at Frankfurt Auto Shows, the first in September 1965 and the new Targa in September 1995, exactly thirty years later.

Little-Known Information

Over the past several years Porsche has worked with Japanese production experts to change the manufacturing process to reduce the number of hours required to build a Porsche. In 1992, it took 125 hours to build one 911, but by 1994 the production time was down to 80 hours. That is one of the main reasons the cost of a Porsche has been reduced. Porsche's next goal is to complete a car in 60 hours.

Porsche 911 America Roadster

In 1952, Porsche introduced a car for the U.S. market called the America Roadster (see page 24). It was designed to be used as a street car, but by removing a few heavy items, the car became very competitive in Sports Car Club of America (SCCA) racing events.

For 1992, the fortieth anniversary of Porsche's first road racing victories in the United States, a new America Roadster was introduced—this time as a 911, available only as a cabriolet. Its body has the wide front and rear flared fenders similar to the 1992 911 Turbo, with the new aerodynamic side-view mirror design. The wheels are also from the Turbo: 7×7 inches in front and 9×17 inches at the rear, with the new five-spoke design. The engine is the 3.6-liter, normally aspirated 6-cylinder from the Carrera, with 247 horsepower at 6,100 rpm; the transmission choices are the five-speed manual or the Tiptronic dual function. The best part is that the brakes and suspension are from the 911 Turbo with independent coil springs at the front and rear. There is a very good chance that the Porsche 911 America Roadster will become a collectible, as the factory has made the decision to limit the number produced to 250 for the 1992 model year. No Porsche convertibles in the United States will have back seats because of the safety regulations mandating rear-seat shoulder belts.

The 1992 America Roadster.

behind! The Tiptronic S transmission (see page 101) has been improved for the new engine output. In the full automatic mode, the transmission automatically downshifts when braking, anticipating the next turn. When in the manual mode, the transmission allows the driver to shift using a floor-mounted stick or a pair of toggle switches on the steering wheel. Of course, no clutch is necessary.

Changes were happening to this 911 Carrera; its look was similar to the 959. The newest of the new features was the suspension. Porsche engineers have taken the fear out of driving a rear-engine car with so much power. The new multilink LSA (Lightweight-Stabile-Agile) suspension is a double wishbone system mounted to a subframe and joined to the body by four rubber bushings at the rear, which minimizes the noise. This new development not only allows a much higher level of precise and predictable handling, but more comfort too. The front suspension is a revised version of the MacPherson strut. The standard wheels are 16-inch-wide rims with Z-rated tires and have been redesigned in cast-aluminum to go with the new body. Options include a sport suspension package with stiffer springs, shock absorbers, and a stiffer and larger-diameter stabilizer bar. Seventeen-inch wheels are optional and a good choice for the sport package.

To add to all this, even the steering wheel has been refitted for the new, smaller airbags, again allowing the driver to use the center of the wheel to blow the horn instead of the small buttons on the earlier model. Even the smallest things—including the windshield wiper system—have been improved. Surprisingly, even with all the new design changes and improvements, the price has actually decreased.

When the Carrera 4 was introduced in 1988, not many Porsche enthusiasts considered an all-wheel drive a high-performance sports car. By the time the 1995 edition was introduced at a much more reasonable price with better performance and drivability, low fuel consumption, and

more flexible handling for the street, customers were looking at it more seriously. The Carrera 4 is identical to the 993 except for the Carrera 4's four-wheel-drive and greater weight (it's 111 pounds [50 kg] heavier than the 993).

The Targa disappeared after 1994 and was reintroduced with the new glass sliding top as a 1996 model. For the new Targa see chapter six (What's New).

The Porsche factory surveys say that 30 percent of the new Porsche buyers are first-time Porsche owners (before 1995 this figure was 17 percent). The female buyer is now 15 percent of their market.

The next event to hold Porsche admirers in thrall was the Boxster (see page 104), introduced in the autumn of 1996.

The 1996 Carrera 911 coupe.

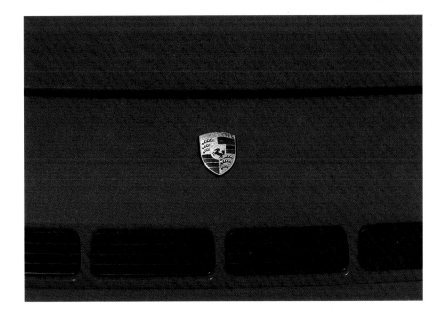

THE 914, 924, 944, AND 968

THE 914S

Porsche has always been successful with its rear-engined race cars as far back as the prewar Auto Unions and into the 1950s and 1960s with the 550 series, RSK, 904, 906, and 908. The design was thought to be the layout of the future for production sports cars.

At the same time that Porsche was considering a new mid-engined car, Heinz Nordhoff, the president of Volkswagen, wanted a sports model to replace the Karmann-Ghia and give the company a sportier image. Nordhoff was a friend of Dr. Ferry Porsche, and talks between them in the 1960s produced an agreement to create the 914 as two separate cars from one body shell. The base model would be the 914/4, a Volkswagen-powered two-seater. The Porsche 914/6 would have a

flat-6 engine that was taken from the 911. The idea was to have Karmann (an independent autobody manufacturing company) supply finished cars to Volkswagen and just bodies of the same design to Porsche in Stuttgart-Zuffenhausen. The most interesting part was that both cars would carry the VW nameplate as well as that of Porsche. It was also decided that in North America only, the cars would be marketed bearing the Porsche badge and sold at the Porsche dealerships.

Unfortunately, during a critical period when the marketing and advertising decisions were being made, Nordhoff passed away. The new Volkswagen president, Kurt Lotz, had different ideas. He did not have much enthusiasm for this new project, especially the part about Porsche selling its own version of the 914. Lotz rejected many of the verbal agreements that had been made

A 914/6 GT racing at the Le Mans 24-hour race in June 1970. Driven by Guy Chasseuil and Claude Ballot-Lena, it won the GT class and came in seventh overall.

between Porsche and Nordhoff. During this transition period, it was decided that Porsche and Volkswagen would enter into a joint venture, with each owning 50 percent of the sales organization that would handle Volkswagen, Porsche, and Audi. This company was now called VW-Porsche VG (Vertriebsgesellschaft) and in the United States was a division of VoA (Volkswagen of America). Dealers could sell all three cars as long as they were in separate operations, and Volkswagens had to be put in a separate facility away from Porsche and Audi.

The first 914s were introduced in September 1969 at the Frankfurt Auto Show, and delivery started in Germany in February 1970. The United States and Canada started receiving cars as late as March. A special appearance group was offered as an option in the standard 914 and 914/6, which included chrome bumpers with driving lights, center console, and vinyl-covered roof pillars with chrome trim. By 1973, the appearance group's center console included gauges and was standard if the 2.0-liter, 4-cylinder engine was ordered.

The standard 914 had the VW 411 sedan engine, as well as four-bolt pattern hubs and wheels. It was built in the Karmann plant when the Karmann-Ghia was no longer in production. The 914/6 had all 911 mechanical components and was completed at the Porsche factory on the same production line as the 911. The brakes, five-bolt pattern hubs, and wheels were all 911 components. The engine used in the 914/6 was the 2.0-liter, 6-cylinder taken from the 1969 911T with triple-throat Weber carburetors, developing 110 horsepower at 5,800 rpm.

The 4-cylinder Porsche had fuel injection to meet the U.S. emissions standards, but by 1975 an air pump was added. The steering rack on both models came from the 911. In addition, the five-speed transmission, as well as portions of the front suspension, came from the 911, but a new rear suspension was designed. It was decided not to use antiroll bars but to work with springs and shocks for its handling characteristics. The weight distribution was about equal, 46 percent of the weight on the front wheels and 54 percent on the rear.

Top: *A 1972 Porsche 914. Virtually unchanged since its introduction as a 1970 model, the subtle changes for 1972 included an adjustable passenger seat and a revised side mirror. Bottom: A 1976 914. This was the last year for the 914, and only the 2.0-liter engine was available. Due to more stringent North American safety regulations, these energy-absorbing bumpers were added in 1975.*

The lift-off fiberglass Targa roof, when removed, fit snugly in the back trunk with enough room left over for a large suitcase. The front trunk housed the spare tire and tool kit. To fill the tank with gasoline, the front trunk had to be opened (like most 356s). Air-conditioning was offered in North America as an option and installed by the dealer. The condenser took away space in the front trunk and under the dash area extra air outlets took away leg room. It also decreased the performance when the compressor kicked in, especially when going uphill.

By the end of 1970, it appeared that the 914/6 was not as popular as the factory thought it would be. The 911T (now with a 2.2-liter engine) was faster and was only slightly higher in price. Production for the following year was cut back. Fewer than 250 models were made for the 1972, its last model year; the 914/6 could be purchased only by special order in North America, and in Germany the only cars available were from remaining inventory. The 914/6 was never a commercial success; a total of 3,360 cars were produced and, sadly, it lasted less than three model years. Today, these cars are very much sought after and command a high price.

The 914/4 continued to be popular, mostly in the United States, as the affordable Porsche from 1970 to 1976. Over 120,000 914s were produced in those six years. Minor changes, such as larger bumpers, adjustable passenger seat, air outlets, more sound-deadening material, and retractable seat belts, upgraded the car each model year. In 1973, the shift linkage was changed and the front rotors were improved. As the U.S. emissions regulations became more stringent, the 4-cylinder engine was increased from 1.7 to 1.8 liters to compensate for the power loss. A year after the demise of the 914/6, a 2.0-liter, 4-cylinder engine was offered to fill the higher performance void that was left.

The great advantage of these mid-engined cars was their compactness; the even weight distribution helped

The 914/8

Experimental cars were always being developed at the engineering offices at Porsche. Sometimes only one car was produced; sometimes, such as in the case of the 914/8, two such cars were built.

The developers of the 914 knew that the chassis could handle 300 horsepower, so Helmutt Bott, the development director of the 914, and Dr. Ferdinand Piëch, the man in charge of Porsche racing efforts at the time, had a flat 8-cylinder engine from the lightweight racing 908 installed in a 914/6 body.

From the exterior, it was hard to tell the difference between the 6 and the 8 except for the opening in the lower half of the front bumper for an extra oil cooler and an exterior fuel-filler cap. It had four Weber twin carburetors and produced 260 horsepower at 7,700 rpm. Its official designation was 914/8 S-II, and one was presented to Dr. Ferry Porsche on his sixtieth birthday. After over 6,000 miles (10,000 kilometers) of driving, it was retired to the Porsche museum because it was too loud to meet the new German noise regulations.

The second 914/8 was built for Dr. Piëch with double retractable headlights. However, the car was never registered for the street and was kept at the test center at Weissach. Today, both cars are at the Porsche museum.

with acceleration, provided better handling, and reduced braking efforts. One of the major disadvantages was the noise factor; since the engine was directly behind the passenger compartment, it was difficult to deaden the sound. This was never a problem with race cars, however, because the driver could always wear ear plugs.

There are a few things potential 914 buyers should keep in mind. First, make sure you check carefully under the

Above: The 1972 Porsche
916, showing its flared
fenders to accommodate
the 7-inch-wide wheels.
Opposite page: The rear
view of the 916, with the
special relief under the
bumper to accommodate
the long European license
plate.

The 916

Because the factory was successfully racing the 914/6 GT, Porsche considered marketing a look-alike car for the street. It was to be Porsche's answer to the Ferrari Dino V-6, and the original plan was to have the introduction at the Paris Salon in mid-October 1971 for the 1972 model year.

Porsche decided that the car would be a deluxe version produced as a limited edition. The engine was from the 911S: 6-cylinder with fuel injection, 190 horsepower at 6,500 rpm, and when combined with a modified five-speed transmission, it could go from 0 to 60 mph (96.5 kph) in under seven seconds. The top speed was 145 mph (233 kph). The exterior body looked much like the racing 914/6 GT, including full fender flares with 15- by 7-inch rims with spacers and 185/70x15 tires, making the track 2 inches wider than the standard 914. Some of the differences from the 914 were the steel roof (welded to the body for extra rigidity), and the fiberglass bumper panels painted the same color as the car, blended with the body at the front and rear. The interior instruments included a combined oil temperature and pressure gauge to the left, a tachometer in the center, and a speedometer on the right. A fuel gauge was added just to the right under the dash. The trim on the seats and door panels was leather, and the seat inserts were a patterned velour to blend with the

carpet and instrument panel: a very unusual combination for Porsche at that time.

The 916 possessed stiff springs with pressurized competition shocks, front and rear swaybars, and four-wheel ventilated disc brakes as standard equipment. It was 165 pounds (75 kg) lighter than the 911S, making it the quickest accelerating street Porsche of its time.

Less than twenty preproduction 916s were built before the decision was made not to go ahead with the project. Some of the reasons behind this decision were the American emissions regulations for the coming year, the fact that the price was more than that of the 911, and the poor performance of the 914/6 in the marketplace.

Several of the 916s were fitted with 8-cylinder engines and have been retained by the factory for its museum. The others went to family members, special distributors, or dealers. Just one was imported into the United States. This car was delivered to Peter Gregg of Brumos Porsche + Audi in Jacksonville, Florida. The factory had a special order to install air-conditioning for that hot and humid climate, making that car the only 916 to leave the Porsche factory with this option. It still resides in Florida and can be seen at vintage races across North America.

battery tray, where acid can drip down and weaken the chassis. Look for rust around the jack points and inside the seams of the rear trunk, where water can sit for weeks. Check to see if the fuel pump has been relocated to a cooler, up-front position; this correction was made by the factory in 1975. The fuel pump was originally located right next to the right heat exchanger, causing vapor lock. Stay away from air-conditioning—with this small engine, the performance will definitely be poor. When shopping for a used 914 today, look for the 2.0-liter models first; they are the most improved and a great buy.

The 914s are great competitors for fun club events such as autocrosses; they are reasonably priced and can be maintained without having to take out a loan. They are enjoyable to drive, even every day, and are good handling cars. But from the beginning, many considered this Porsche a Volkswagen and never accepted the model. These same skeptics seem to forget that the first Porsche started as a Volkswagen.

THE 924, 924S, AND 924 TURBO

In late 1975, a new Porsche, the 924, was introduced as a 1976 model for the European market. Other countries did not see the new car until 1976 as a 1977 model. By July 1977, the end of the first full production year, 23,180 cars had left the factory, making the 924 the most successful model ever produced by the company. The 924 was the first front-engined, water-cooled Porsche to reach the public; even though the 928 had started its development earlier (see chapter five), all other Porsches to date had air-cooled engines, always placed somewhere behind the driver. The reason for the change was simple: the 924 was designed by Porsche to be a Volkswagen and ended up a Porsche.

A 1978 Porsche 924. This was the first year for the optional five-speed transmission in Germany.

When the joint venture of VW-Porsche VG was formed to market the 914, it became apparent that this car was not going to last. Since VW management still wanted a car to give Volkswagen that sporty image, it contracted with Porsche to design an automobile using VW parts for high-volume manufacturing, with a high comfort level, including more passenger space than in the 914, and a front-engine design. It was agreed upon that the air-cooled engine was on its way out, so a new water-cooled design was chosen. The car was to be sold as a VW/Audi.

In 1973, before production began, the VG company dissolved, but Volkswagen still wanted to produce the car that they had financed; they also felt that Volkswagen should market the car, since Volkswagen had a much larger dealer network than VW-Porsche. But then the

1973 to 1974 oil embargo occurred, and Volkswagen was not so sure it could sell an upscale car. A combination of corporate policy changes and personnel replacements led to the entire project being bought back by Porsche from Volkswagen. When VW considered closing its plant in Neckarsulm, West Germany, one of eight factories, it was decided that the new 924 would be built there by Porsche. The 924s, and later the 944s, continued to be manufactured at the Neckarsulm factory.

This new budget car would now be called a Porsche, but enthusiasts found it hard to accept. The styling was very new for Porsche, with lots of glass and more interior space than any of the other models. The 924 had VW brakes, steering, suspension, and a VW engine in design, but the car was fully developed, tested, and built by

Audi. The same 4-cylinder engine was used in the VW LT van, and in the American Motors Gremlin with a carburetor instead of fuel injection. It produced 125 horsepower for the British and European markets, but only 95 horsepower for North America and Japan, due to their tighter emissions regulations. By 1977, the horsepower was increased to 110 on North American models, with a new designation of 1977½.

Other differences between the European and the North American versions were the side marker lights (even today the location of these marker lights will differ between cars in Europe and North America) and the front and rear bumpers, which had to be changed to meet safety regulations.

A roller shade was installed at midyear 1977, to hide luggage in the rear, and the automatic transmission was also offered as an alternative to the car's original four-speed manual transmission. This was the first Porsche to have a fully automatic transmission. The new Porsche also had fuel injection.

Because of the engine at the front of the 924, the transmission was located at the rear, creating a more equal weight distribution (48 percent in the front and 52 percent in the rear). By the 1977 Frankfurt Auto Show, a new five-speed option was offered for the 1978 model year (standard in 1979), which, in addition to its outstanding handling characteristics, made the car much more fun to drive. The headlights were raised and lowered by electric motors, and the rear hatchback lifted for storage access. The 2+2 back seats were slightly larger than those in the 911, but were only comfortable for two adults on short trips. It was great for kids because they were forced to stay in one place. The back seats also folded down to increase the luggage area.

From its introduction, the motor press did not like the noise that the 924 produced. The early cars had a suspension vibration that was corrected by 1978. The other fault was that the steering wheel did not have adequate clearance in a turn when the driver's hands were in the 3 and 9 o'clock position. But the 924 was getting close to becoming the car that Porsche wanted it to be, and its production exceeded 50,000 cars in just twenty-six months.

The market for this car in Great Britain had a deluxe package that included alloy wheels, headlight washers, rear window wiper, and tinted glass, which were all included in the base price. The rest of the world had two Touring Packages to choose from, offered as options at an additional cost. The additional options for all markets included air-conditioning, a removable roof panel, metallic paint, front and rear antiroll bars, and three radio speakers with an antenna.

For the North American market, the Martini Edition (1977) and the Sebring '79 Special Edition (in the United States only) were introduced bearing a special paint job with logo and alloy wheels, and were produced as a limited edition. In the European market, a special Le Mans edition was introduced to celebrate the three finishes of the 924 Carrera GTRs at the 24-Hours of Le Mans in France. (See page 85.)

The 924 was said to be a very practical Porsche. It was economical to run, and its fuel consumption was reasonable. An article in the British publication, *Thoroughbred & Classic Cars* stated, "If you want a Porsche and can't afford a 911, then this is a very good compromise that in feel appears to owe nothing to the VW connection—it is a real Porsche."

The news for 1979 was the 924 Turbo, a car built by Porsche. The engines were still assembled at Neckarsulm on the same assembly line as the 924, but they were trucked to Porsche's works in Zuffenhausen, where the Turbo components were added. The way to identify this new quick Porsche was by the functional NACA air duct on the front hood, four air-intake slots above the front bumper, newly designed alloy wheels, gravel guards at

the rear, and front and rear spoilers. The first Turbos that came to North America had a very unusual black and white checkered flag fabric on the seat inserts and door panels. This same pattern was also seen on early 928s, but fortunately for the buying public, it did not last very long.

The horsepower on the 924 Turbo was 170 at 5,500 rpm in the European market and 143 at 5,500 rpm in the North American market. The 924 Turbo weighed 60 pounds (27 kg) more than the 924, requiring adjustments including stiffer shocks, heavier antiroll bars, and recalibrated front springs due to its increased performance. Porsche continued to add extras each year, including rear seat belts, extra soundproofing, suspension improvements, and halogen headlights. In 1981, the Turbo was modified and four-wheel disc brakes became standard on both the 924 and 924 Turbo. The 924s were never quite respected as a Porsche in the North American market, but that same market was ready for the 924 Turbo they had heard about in all the automotive magazines. The Turbo was discontinued in the summer of 1982, except for a small number for the Italian market.

Other variations of the 924 included: in 1979, a Carrera GT for racing (only four hundred were made to satisfy Group 4 homologation requirements of FISA [Federation Internationale Sportif Automobile]); in 1980, a 924D (a special kit for SCCA "D Production"); also in 1980, a 924 Carrera Le Mans GT "P" (specially built prototypes for the 1980 Le Mans race with 917 brakes); a Carrera GTS for Group 4 competition; a Rally Package with higher ground clearance, heavy-duty suspension, and an antiroll bar; and, in 1981, the Carrera GTS for Group 4 and Trans-Am racing.

At the Frankfurt Auto Show in September 1981, an all-new Porsche was introduced: the 944. During this time, the 924 and 924 Turbo were taken off the market in North America, but they continued to be produced for

Europe and the United Kingdom with an updated interior. In February 1982, the 100,000th 924 came off the production line.

In 1986, for the 1987 model year, the 924 was upgraded for all markets, and a new 924S was introduced as the latest entry-level Porsche. This new car was built with 944 brakes, electrical system, suspension, and drivetrain. The engine was also straight from the 944, but in the lighter 924 body. The car possessed air-conditioning, tinted glass, heated power-remote mirrors, power steering, power windows, and a power antenna as standard equipment. The new S was as fast as the 944 Turbo when flat out and could rival the Turbo in acceleration. A bargain Porsche, optional equipment for it included a radio/tape player, limited-slip differential, automatic transmission, electric sunroof, and a rear window wiper. Porsche chose to discontinue this car at the end of 1988.

Opposite page: A 1981 924 Carrera GTS. When introduced, this was the fastest 4-cylinder road car in the world. Although not allowed on public roads in North America, it was street legal in Germany. Above: A 1980 Porsche Turbo "Le Mans," a prototype specially built for the Le Mans 24-Hour endurance race. It used the brakes and centerlock wheels from the larger, faster race cars.

THE 944, 944S, AND 944 TURBO

Although the arrival of the 944 was announced in 1981 in Europe, it was not officially introduced to the North American market until May 1982 as a 1983 model. The U.S. dealers received so many advance orders that there was a six-month waiting list for delivery. The reason for all the delays was that the engine had not been fully tested: Porsche wanted to be sure this engine was a true Porsche product. Porsche had to please the buying public and especially wanted the automotive press to give the car high marks.

The 944 had a 2.5-liter engine by Porsche, revised bodywork, and a great price. The standard options available on this model were the same as other models.

It was said that the 944's engine was half of the 928 V–8, but this was never true. However, the technology gained from the 928 power plant was transferred to the development of this new 4-cylinder. The European horsepower was 160 at 5,800 rpm and the North American cars had 143 horsepower at 5,500 rpm. To keep the noise level down, which had been a problem with the 924, the engineers used a special balance-shaft design that they paid Mitsubishi a patent fee to use. Porsche also worked on other factors to quiet the ride and succeeded.

The chassis and body shell of the 944 were from the 924, but the fenders were flared (resembling the 924 Carrera GT race car) for the wider tires and wheels. A front air dam was added and a rear spoiler attached to the bottom of the hatchback window. As with the 924, the steering wheel still did not leave adequate clearance between the driver's hands and legs when in a turn. This problem was later addressed by lowering the seats, raising the steering wheel, and offering a smaller steering wheel as an option. This car was finally a Porsche's Porsche. It was everything that the 924 should have been.

Opposite page: *This 1983 Porsche 944 had a sunroof and fog lights as standard equipment. The sunroof was operated by removing the steel panel and storing it in a special bag in the hatchback trunk.*
Left: *A 1984 944.*

In 1985, the interior of the 944 was completely changed, with a new dash design and a rearranged instrument panel for better viewing. The factory figures state that the 944 could go from 0 to 60 (96.5 kph) in 8.3 seconds with a top speed of 130 mph (109 kph). The 924 Turbo would reach 0 to 60 mph (96.5 kph) in 9.1 seconds. Now how fast could a 944 Turbo fly?

At a top speed of over 150 mph (241 kph) with 217 horsepower at 5,800 rpm, the 944 Turbo, introduced at the end of 1985, was definitely a fast runner. It had excellent high-end range and could go from 0 to 60 mph (96.5 kph) in 6.1 seconds. The Turbo's outer skin differed from that of the normally aspirated model, with a revised nose with wide slots for cooling and a rear underbody pan for better high-speed stability. A front and rear spoiler and wider wheels and tires were included. The wheels that were used had the five-hole design, sometimes called "phone dial" wheels, copied from the early 928s.

In Germany in 1986, the Porsche 944 Turbo Cup racing series was introduced, featuring near-standard models with catalytic converters and 220 horsepower (increased to 250 horsepower by the following year). A new "sports" suspension kit became available as an option for street cars following the Turbo Cup racing developments. The factory announced in 1987, for the 1988 model year, a special edition of 1,000 models of the Turbo S to be produced to similar specifications as the Turbo Cup series cars.

By mid-1986, a newer 944 was announced: the 944S. The major change was the engine; it now had twin-cams and four valves per cylinder, similar to the 928S4 in technology, but with no interchangeable parts. The horse-

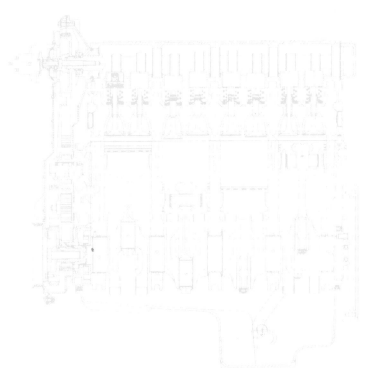

Right: *A cutaway view of the basic 2.5-liter, 4-cylinder Porsche 944 engine. Designed and built entirely by Porsche, it has been enlarged and modified since its introduction to deliver more power, as well as to meet ever more stringent emissions regulations worldwide.* **Bottom:** *A 1987 944. ABS (antilock braking system) was available on the 944 for the first time in 1987.*

power was now raised to 188 at 6,000 rpm and the top speed was over 140 mph (225 kph). By 1987, both the 944 Turbo and the 944S now had ABS (antilock braking system) as an option (standard on all models in 1989). Air bags were standard on the Turbo for both the driver and the passenger and were optional on the 944 and 944S. Porsche was the first automotive manufacturer that offered air bags for the passenger, optional or standard.

Porsche added more standard equipment to the cars each year, and by 1988, this included air-conditioning, power windows and locks, a rear spoiler, electric height adjustment for the driver's seat, heated rear window, and an indicator that sensed the brake-pad wear.

Porsche always added limited edition models to its lines. These cars were made with special treatment, and they also had special features. One such special edition car was called a 944 TurboS, only 700 of which were

built in 1988. The engine had 30 more horsepower than the regular Turbo and went from 0 to 60 mph (96.5 kph) in 5.5 seconds, with a top speed of 162 mph (261 kph). The suspension was designed with stiffer springs, the shock absorbers were firmer, and the antiroll bars were heavier in order to control this higher-performance street car.

There were a lot of Porsches to pick from, in a wide range of prices, in 1989. The 944S was replaced by the 944 S2, with a new 3.0-liter engine now up to 208 horsepower. A new 944 S2 cabriolet, the car Porsche enthusiasts had been awaiting for over three years, was ready for delivery. There were also more standard equipment items, including cruise control, a removable electric sunroof, and an alarm system that blinked a light in the top of the door lock when engaged. The least expensive car in the line was the 944.

The 944, 944 S2, and 944 Turbo were all available in 1989. By 1990 there was only the 944S2 in a coupe or cabriolet. In 1989, the last year that the 944 Turbo was produced, the turbocharger was increased in size and the horsepower was up to 247 at 6,000 rpm. The new car that replaced the 944 was the 968 for the 1992 model year, a car said to be close to the 911 Carrera.

THE 968

The latest from Porsche in 1992 was the 968, which replaced the ten-year-old 944. It was the least expensive of all the Porsches.

Porsche promoted the 968 at its introduction as an 80 percent newly designed car. The transmission had six speeds, with sixth gear being slightly "longer" than fifth. Both fifth and sixth were overdrive gears. For the automatic, Porsche used a four-speed Tiptronic revised from the transmission used on the Carrera 2. This was also the year that all automatic-transmissioned cars coming into North America had to have a shiftlock, so drivers could

not take out the ignition key unless the shift lever was in park. Another safety feature would not let the driver move the shift lever out of park unless the brake pedal was depressed.

If you looked at the 968 from the front, you could see some of the 911 lines above the hood. The pop-up headlights and front fenders raised into the hoodline look like they were taken from the 928, with a little 959 angling thrown in. The roofline is from the 944, as is the rear glass. The doors have that 944 look, and the fog lights integrated in the bumpers resemble the 928 after a diet. The interior door panels appear to be taken from the 911.

Porsche was never one for wasting leftover parts from the last model. They used the 356 engines in the early 912s and the 914 2.0-liter engines in the 912Es. Even the door handles from the early 911s showed up on the next model until they were used up.

The horsepower changed from 208 at 5,800 rpm on the 944 to 236 at 6,200 rpm on the 968. The torque

The 1991 944 S2 Cabriolet, with its 3.0-liter engine, produced 208 horsepower at 5,800 rpm.

The 1992 968 was available as a coupe or cabriolet. The 3.0-liter 4-cylinder engine produced 236 horsepower at 6,200 rpm.

was increased from 207 to 225 foot-pounds at 4,100 rpm, the highest for any normally aspirated 3.0-liter engine. This engine still had only four cylinders.

After using the same chassis from the 944 Turbo, Porsche revised the springs, shocks, and antiroll bras. If the customer preferred a harder ride and more rubber on the road, a special handling package could be ordered as an option. This sports suspension package included 17-inch aluminum wheels with wider front and rear tires. The suspension included stiffer springs, adjustable shock absorbers, larger brakes, and a device that adjusted the ride height.

The view from the rear of the car shows "968" in raised numbers above the embossed PORSCHE lettering. The bumpers were integrated into the body to give a beautiful uninterrupted flow. The light alloy wheels were the new five-spokes that were seen before on the 911 Turbo, and the aerodynamic side-view mirrors (also from the 911 Turbo) appear on all models.

Highlights from the 968 interior included the 944 dash, with a few gauges changed around. The clock was moved to the center of the console; a digital temperature read-out took up the old clock position. The top track speed was 156 mph (251 kph), compared to 149 mph (240 kph) for the 944. However, the speedometer reads up to 180 mph (288 kph), perhaps to accommodate future advances in engine design. According to the manufacturer's data, the acceleration was from 0 to 60 mph (96.5 kph) in 6.1 seconds with the manual transmission and 7.5 seconds with Tiptronic.

Because the 968 was built in Zuffenhausen, special orders could be easily handled; paint could even be swatched. Just pick out your best color, maybe from your favorite tie; Porsche will match it and paint your car to order.

One of the fun options is the remote CD player. You put the discs in the trunk-mounted system, select your plays from your seat, and listen from ten speakers hidden throughout the interior.

The 968 was available in the coupe (with a rear spoiler) and the cabriolet—two very attractive options. The convertibles coming to North America had no backseats because of the safety regulations mandating rear-seat shoulder belts, but the European model had the small seats like the 944 cabriolet. Backseat or no backseat, my choice still would be the convertible, especially with the new power-assisted and easy-to-operate top. The old design from the early Targa was finally updated.

When adding it all up, the 968 was quicker, stopped in less time, had greater handling, and was a better all-around Porsche than the 944.

The 968 was the most affordable Porsche since the company's inception. By 1994, new exterior colors were available, and the seats and wheels had been restyled. During this model year the optional new Torsen™ torque-sensing differential was introduced, replacing the conventional limited-slip differential option on cars equipped with the six-speed transmission.

Porsche stopped producing the 968 in 1995.

Special Editions

Every so often, to keep the attention of the Porsche buyer, the factory will introduce a special edition Porsche that has some extra features over the basic line and that is limited in the number produced. The changes offered on these specials and their limited production adds to the rarity of the model and helps to hold the model's value.

The 911 SC Weissach Coupe

Only 400 of the exclusive limited edition 911SC Weissach Coupes were made. They were almost sold out before they reached the North American shores. The car was basically a 1980 SC with all the standard features: a flat-6, horizon- tally opposed, 3.0-liter engine, 172 horsepower at 5,500 rpm. It could reach 0 to 60 mph (96.5 kph) in 6.5 seconds in second gear, with a top speed of 140 mph (225 kph). The added goodies included a functional spoiler under the nose and a "whale tail" spoiler at the rear (last seen on the 911 Turbo). During high-speed driving, these spoilers stabilized the car; they also made it look fast in traffic.

The other additions included sports shocks and special Pirelli CN36 tires. There were special sealed-beam halogen headlights (the U.S. regulations at the time required sealed beams), an electric antenna, rear speakers (the radio was extra), and electrically heated mirrors on both sides (only one was standard).

These cars were available in only two colors: black or champagne gold. The wheels were forged alloy with plat- inum metallic centers with the Porsche crest. The interior was light beige leather with contrasting burgundy piping on the seats, and the floor had plush burgundy carpeting— a very attractive combination.

Lower left: The rugged Porsche forged-aluminum alloy wheels were standard equipment on the 911SC Weissach Coupes. First introduced on the new 1967 911S, they steadily grew in width to accommodate improvements in suspension and tire technology. Lower right: In 1980, the center console, the three-spoke, 15-inch (38-cm) steering wheel, and electric windows all became standard on the 911 models. Seen here is the Weissach Coupe's light beige leather interior with con- trasting burgundy piping.

The Martini, the Sebring '79, and the Le Mans

A Martini Edition 924 was produced for sale in the spring of 1977, celebrating two world championship crowns earned by Porsche the year before in Group 5 and Group 6 racing. All the cars were painted white with the Martini stripes on both sides. The interior included deep red pile carpets and trim changes.

The Sebring '79 was produced for the U.S. market, with a total of 1,300 cars painted bright orange-red. The script lettering "Sebring 79" was written in white on the front fender, under the black, white, and gold striping on the side, like the pace car at the famous 12-Hours of Sebring (Florida) race.

A Le Mans edition was introduced later for the European market, honoring the three 1980 finishes by Porsche 924 Carrera GTRs (sixth, twelfth, and thirteenth) at the famous 24-hour race in France. These cars were painted white, with gold, red, and black striping on the side. The word "Le Mans" was lettered on the front fender. As many as one hundred of these special edition Porsches were sent to England, and only a few reached the Australian shores because of the quota system in place there.

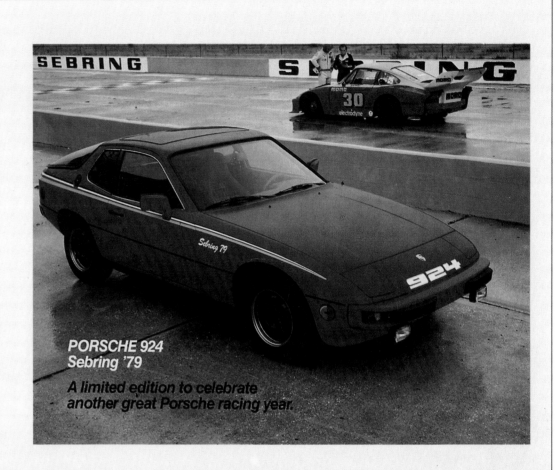

PORSCHE 924
Sebring '79
A limited edition to celebrate another great Porsche racing year.

The 924 Weissach

The 924 Weissach special edition was designed for the purpose of encouraging the sale of more cars. This model was available only in metallic platinum, which looked close to a metallic light brown. Only a limited number were produced for the North American market in 1981. Featuring special wheels and the rear spoiler from the Turbo, it was a very strong-looking car.

The 928 Weissach Special Edition

This special model 928 followed in the tradition of other Weissach specials, with a limited production of only 205 cars. Mechanically, everything was the same. The difference was in the champagne gold metallic paint scheme with the matching brushed gold-colored alloy wheels—a beautiful combination. A spoiler was added to the rear hatchback window and another to the lower front of the nose. The interior included an electric sunroof, a digital radio, and special two-toned leather throughout. The best addition was the three-piece Porsche luggage set that was made from the same leather as the interior. If you happen to get the chance to buy one of these special edition 928s, I wonder if the luggage will still be part of the deal!

Opposite page: The 911SC Weissach Coupe offered as a special edition in 1980. Above: To commemorate their victories at Sebring in 1979, Porsche offered a special limited edition "Sebring '79" 924 in the United States market.

CHAPTER FIVE

THE 928

Pages 86 and 87: A 1982 Porsche 928. Right: In the foreground, a complete rear end with an automatic transmission destined for a 928 awaits the final assembly line. The smaller casing is the five-speed manual transmission.

riginally called Project 928, the Porsche 928 was introduced at the Geneva Automobile Salon in March 1977. The original idea for the 928 took place during the early 1970s, when the people at Porsche were thinking about a possible successor to the famous 911. It had been a concern for many years that the 911 buyer might just suddenly stop buying; with more than half of its production coming to the United States, Porsche had to seriously consider that market. But it is also quite possible that the development of the new 928 had nothing to do with replacing the 911, and that the factory wanted to prove that it could build a car with a water-cooled engine that was in front, rather than air-cooled and mounted in the rear.

The engineers knew that a new car from Porsche had to be new from the ground up, and that was how the project worked from beginning to end. Every part was designed from scratch. About halfway through the project the world had an energy crisis, which quickly changed some of the thinking at Porsche. But the project continued with better ideas for a more energy-conscious buyer. Since the car was created from the drawing board, it did not have to resemble any other Porsche, and the new car definitely looked different. We are now used to the design, but in 1977, many thought of it as strange, unusual, futuristic, even spaceship-looking. But, the question at the time was: would the traditional Porsche fan have interest in this new front-engined, water-cooled car? As it turned out, a new kind of Porsche buyer purchased this trendy car. In 1992, the 928 S4 (four-speed automatic) and GT (five-speed manual transmission) were offered. The 928 GTS is the newest model in this line.

When the new 928 was first driven by the motor press of the world, it received many outstanding awards. They called it the new breed of supercar.

THE DEVELOPMENT

Starting from scratch was the best challenge: the ideas were limitless, but the demands heavy. The new car had to be able to accommodate future regulations, and it had to stand the test of time, as the 356 and 911 had. The 356 series had continued for fifteen years. By 1977, the year of the 928's introduction, the 911 was already in its thirteenth year, with no end in sight.

The original idea for the 928 was on the drawing boards by 1971, and after a frantic race for time, a completed skeleton model was ready by 1972, followed by the unveiling of a full-scale model in the fall of the next year.

The first change from other Porsches was the engine. A 6-cylinder was considered, but it was decided that the engine definitely had to be performance-oriented, keeping with the company's image, and there had to be room for expansion. Another major requirement was the ability to meet future legislation for emissions. The final decision was a water-cooled 90-degree V-8.

Top: *A 1978 Porsche 928. The most advanced feature was the Weissach rear axle, which automatically adjusted to the driver's input, thus creating great confidence in the car's handling abilities. Lower left: A 928 receives its paint in a special ventilated paint booth. The painter removed his mask for this photograph. Bottom right: A worker begins to install the driver's seat track in a 928. The extra-large transmission hump identifies this as an automatic model, which requires different rear seats than the smaller five-speed manual model.*

Top left: *The rear of a 928 S4.* **Bottom right:** *The 928 headlights are retracted when not in use. The headlight pictured is a standard sealed beam for the North American market. The small nozzle located in the bumper below the headlight sprays water on the headlights for cleaning.*

Deciding where to build the car was the next problem. The factory at Stuttgart-Zuffenhausen, where over 13,000 911s were being produced, estimated that 5,000 928s could be produced. They switched some of the 911 production over to 928. The total capacity was 20,000 a year.

THE LOOK, THE FEEL, THE IMAGE, THE 928

Look at the bumpers—the car looks like it has none. This is because the design engineers integrated the polyurethane-paneled bumpers into the body and carefully painted the body and bumpers to match. To keep the car from getting overweight, the V-8 engine, doors, front hood, and fenders were made of aluminum. Porsche had to find new paint adhesions for the steel, aluminum, and polyurethane, for all had to look equal in color and be long-lasting.

The headlights of the 928 are set into the body, raised by an electric motor. The North American version has both high and low beams in one set of lights. In Europe the pop-up lights are only for the low beams, and the high-beam lights are set into the front bumper; on those cars, the headlight height adjustment can be changed with a knob on the floor next to the driver's thigh.

When sitting in the driver's seat, you get the feeling you can actually fly. The instrument panel has the appearance of the interior of an airplane. The whole instrument cluster moves up and down along with the steering wheel so the driver can see all the dials all the time. Even the pedal positions are adjustable. The electrically adjustable outside mirrors are heated for humid or icy days and nights. The secure design of the interior puts the driver and passengers in a safety cocoon. The rear seating (2+2), does not have enough room for an adult on a cross-country trip but is adequate for young children or short rides when the front seats are in the mid-position. The back seats also fold down separately to add more space in the hatchback trunk area.

The handling is definitely quick; the 50-50 weight distribution was accomplished by mounting the engine in the front, with the combined gearbox and final drive assembly in the rear. The famous Weissach rear axle,

A 1980 Porsche 928. The optional climate control and sunroof were the two most important changes from 1979.

Opposite page: *For 1984, the Porsche 928S was the only 928 model offered. The engine had been enlarged to 4.6 liters, and a new four-speed automatic transmission, supplied by Daimler-Benz, was available as an option.* Top left: *The interior of a 1984 Porsche 928S. The steering wheel adjusts up and down, and the instrument panel moves along with it, allowing the driver to see the instruments at all times.* Top right: *The rear seats of the 928 fold down to expand the rear storage area.*

named after the Porsche Research and Development Center in Weissach, Germany, keeps the car under control in all conditions and, as one 928 car owner once claimed, it keeps the driver out of trouble.

By 1979, even the radio was standard on the 928. The only extras that were available included an alarm system, power seats, limited-slip differential, and a partial leather interior. Another plus was the dual rear sun visors to keep the sun from penetrating the large hatchback window. The European engine was 240 bhp at 5,250 rpm, and the North American version was 225 bhp equipped with catalytic converters. The 928's less expensive competition was the Jaguar XJS and the Ferrari 308GT4—if your Ferrari order had been placed the year before! In Australia a quota restricted the importation of Porsche 928s to fifty a year, and there was a delivery delay of up to fourteen months. Sometimes it is hard to get what you really want, but definitely worth the wait.

When the gas crunch hit in 1979, it looked like the fast sports cars would be lost forever; but over thirteen years later, we are still surprised by Ferrari, Lotus, Alfa-Romeo, Jaguar, Mercedes, and Porsche. Gone are MG, Triumph, and Lancia to mention a few.

When inflation hit in 1980, many of the standard equipment items on the cars from the previous year became optional. Customers had to pay extra for the weather group that included a rear wiper, two-stage windshield washer, and headlight washers. The car was available to the U.S., Canadian, and Japanese markets as a 928, but in Europe it was marketed as a 928S. This designation was not used until 1983 in the North American markets. The exterior changes included a small spoiler under the nose and another around the tail. The rubbing strip along the sides was added to protect the aluminum doors from other car doors. The wheels had a new flat design with the Porsche crest in the center. The engine went from 4.5 to 4.7 liters (by 1985 it was increased again to 5.0 liters). The interior had a new four-spoke steering wheel covered in leather, and the center armrest console incorporated a hidden cassette holder.

Every year Porsche made some change, even if it was only minor. By 1985, the 928S was coming of age with the new twin-cam cylinder heads with four valves per cylinder. The marketing department, concerned about keeping the North American buyer, decided to introduce the new 5.0-liter engine there that year. The production figures for 1985 were 5,356, but by 1986 they were down to 4,617, some of the decline having to do with the higher cost. But even though the car became more expensive, many of the optional items of the year before were now standard equipment, such as the ABS braking system. Other new additions were the windshield radio antenna incorporated into the glass and an added warranty program that covered the power train for 50,000 miles (80,000 km) and extended the rust coverage from seven to ten years.

In 1987, the 928 S4 (the "4" standing for the four camshafts) was available in all markets, and the production figures were up to 5,403. The body was redesigned to include a new front, which incorporated fog and driving lights in the nose and a new spoiler with rectangular slits to add cooling to the engine and brakes. The rear had a new larger wing for reduced lift and air resistance at high speeds and a complete change in the rear taillight design that made everything flush with the bumper. Acceleration was 0 to 60 mph (96.5 km) in 5.7 seconds. A Club Sport was also available in a lightweight version with no air-conditioning, with even better acceleration. Porsche states the top speed as 165 mph (265 kph), but Al Holbert, in a stock 928 S4 including a catalytic converter, set an FIA international speed record at the Bonneville Salt Flats at 171.110 mph (275.316 kph) for the flying mile.

One of the negative aspects of the car was the original air-conditioning. With so much glass, it was difficult to keep the interior cool on hot sunny days. Porsche addressed this problem in later models with an additional air-conditioning system between the back seats, including separate air outlets.

The new 32-valve, 5.0-liter 928S engine was first introduced to the North American market in Arizona in 1985.

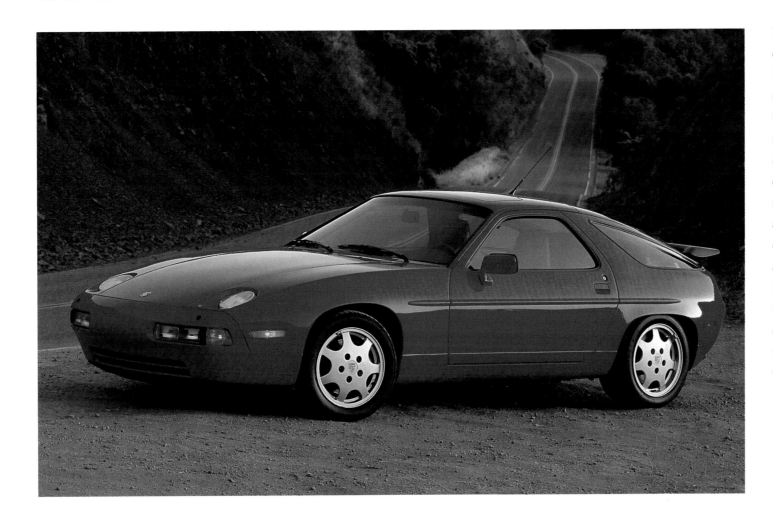

The designation "S4" for automatic transmission or "GT" for five-speed manual transmission is displayed on the rear of the 1991 928. In the 1990 model year, Porsche became the world's first automobile manufacturer to make driver and passenger side airbags standard equipment on every vehicle sold in North America. Today, Porsche is the only manufacturer to offer driver and passenger side airbags in every one of its models worldwide.

The base price of the car included lots of extras. One of the options was a seat position memory system that included the adjustment of the outside mirrors; it recalled three separate adjustments. For an additional charge per seat, it could adjust the lumbar support, allowing you to move it into position and angle it horizontally or vertically in order to relieve back stress. Heated seats were another option available on this car.

In the late 1980s, a weak dollar made it very difficult for Porsche to compete in the North American market. The final production figure at the end of 1988 was 3,663, the following year 2,919, but it went up again in 1990 to 3,088.

The end of the 1980s saw few changes, but in 1990, the power was again increased, though only in the man-

ual transmission. The automatic was 316 horsepower at 6,000 rpm, and the manual was up to 326 at 6,200 rpm, top speed being 165 and 171 mph (265 and 275 kph)— very exciting for a street car. The engine also included a knock sensor, allowing the car to run on different grades of unleaded fuels. One of the new features was an alert display on the instrument panel: when a tire loses pressure it alerts the driver by a light and digital read-out—it even lets the driver know which tire is low. One interesting goody was the air-conditioned glove compartment.

For 1991, the options available were special soft leather seat upholstery for the front and rear (regular leather was standard), a compact disc player, all sorts of seat options (including sports seats with electric height adjustment for driver and passenger), and heated seats.

The three-position memory seat and outside mirrors were standard for the driver, but an option for the passenger.

Since 1990, dual air bags have been standard on all Porsches. In 1995 the 928GTS provided three-point safety belts for both front and rear passengers. The digital display stereo cassette radio now had ten speakers instead of the standard four of the early cars. The list goes on, including an alarm system and an electric sun-roof. The price was still under the 911 Turbo, a Ferrari, or a Countach.

The S4 (automatic) and GT (five-speed) were not changed for 1992. New for North America in 1993, but already introduced to Europe since 1992, was the 928 GTS. What separated it from the S4 and the ST models were the flared wheel arches to accept the wider Turbo-design 17-inch wheels. The reflective rear panel between the taillights was also new. The standard 5.0-liter engine had been expanded to 5.4 liters, improving the horse-power to 345, with 0 to 60 mph (96.5 kph) in 5.5 seconds with the five-speed manual transmission; the four speed automatic version went from 0 to 60 mph (96.5 kph) in 5.6 seconds. Top track speed for both was 171 mph (275 kph).

Beginning with the 1993 models, Porsche started using the new CFC-free refrigerant, HGC-134a, in the air-conditioning systems. To keep the 928 customer coming back, many of the options from previous years were added as standard equipment on the 1994 and 1995 models without increasing the sticker prices.

The Porsche 928 GTS could be ordered with the Porsche Pocket Commander cellular telephone, developed to be free of interference from the vehicle's electronic system, and can be retrofitted to older Porsches. The best option of all continues to be the option to order your Porsche, pick it up at the German factory, sample the high-speed European motorways and scenic sideroads, then have your car shipped home.

Porsche stopped producing the 928 in 1995.

CHAPTER SIX

WHAT IS NEW FROM PORSCHE?

As of July 1995, when the factory in Germany closed down for summer vacation, production of the water-cooled 968 and 928 had already ceased. The new line consists of seven models: the 911 Carrera Coupe and Cabriolet, the 911 Carrera 4 Coupe and Cabriolet, the 911 Carrera 4S, the 911 Targa, and the 911 Turbo. The new Porsche and much-awaited model was the Boxster, introduced in the autumn of 1996.

The Targa–Glass Top 911

After discontinuing the 968 and 928 models, Porsche debuted a new idea in the 911 Targa, intended to keep the customers coming into the showroom. This new design looked nothing like the Targa that was first intro-duced in 1965 with the lateral roll bar and removable roof. This new Targa appeared to have an entire roof of glass; the roof actually has steel beams on either side of the glass roof module to provide rollover protection. The glass slides from the top of the windshield to the back of the engine compartment in the rear. If you don't like people peering through the tinted glass roof when waiting at a traffic light, there is a roller hidden in the roof lining above the sun visor that becomes an opaque black headliner.

The new look is spectacular and the driving experience even more so. The all-around visibility is superb with or without the roof closed. To open the roof there is no need to stop the car; you just hit a switch and the wind deflector rises. Hit another switch and the roof slides under the rear window. The roof can be opened a few

inches or all the way. A special rubber seal drains any moisture from the roof when the window slides back. The best part is the visibility—the "surround-sound" concept has been applied to the view. The other added plus is the headroom. If you've had difficulty with lack of headroom in sunroofed cars because of the resulting lowered head-liner, then try the new Targa. There is no headliner and there may even be enough space for a cowboy hat!

The "Varioram" System

For the 1996 911 (type 993) models, Porsche boosted its power and torque output with a new "Varioram" system (variable induction system). The horsepower increased

from 270 to 282 and the torque changed from 243 to 250 foot-pounds, but the best increase came in the mid-range torque (up to 18 percent). If you have a place to drive at the top speed of 171 mph (275 kph) (or even if you don't) this new system will bring you up to speed with a lot more kick.

Tiptronic S—Better than Automatic

The driver can choose a manual or fully automatic drive mode with the Tiptronic S gearbox—it puts fun into deci-sion making without a clutch. For 1995, there is a steering-wheel option, which toggles up for a higher gear or down for a lower gear. Switches on both the right and the left accommodate right- or left-handed drivers. A floor-mounted stick remains, and can be used whenever the mood strikes. The transmission can also be put into automatic to let the Porsche do the deciding. This Tiptronic transmission is not available for the Carrera 4 or the Turbo.

Left: Notice the Tiptronic S switches on the right and left sides of the steering wheel—these accommodate both left- and right-handed drivers. Above: A cutaway drawing of the 1993 Carrera 2 with the Tiptronic transmission.

The Carrera 4S Widebody

Porsche now offers a Turbo-look version of the all-wheel-drive Carrera 4 but with the retractable rear spoiler instead of the Turbo's fixed rear wing. This model comes with the flared rear fenders, front air-dam, and 18-inch turbo-look wheels in pressure-cast alloy. The front wheels are 8 inches and the rears are 10 inches wide. Brakes are the same as on the Turbo, and the suspension is the same as the Carrera 4. You can special-order such options as a sport chassis, which includes stiffer springs, larger stabilizer bars, and custom-tuned shock absorbers. This model is available in the coupe only.

The 911 Turbo

The ads for the new Turbo read "Kills bugs fast." With a top speed of 181 mph (291 kph) and an acceleration rate of 0 to 60 mph (96.5 kph) in just over four heartbeats (who's counting heartbeats?), the Turbo is definitely bad news for the insect world.

The planned production for 1996 Porsches for North America is 6,000, of which 800 are to be Turbos (see page 57 for the Turbo history).

Opposite: The 1996 Porsche 911 Turbo, with its 400 horsepower, revised suspension, and all-wheel drive, is the fastest, most competent production automobile in North America, and is almost as ferocious as the trendsetting 959. With its state-of-the-art ABS 5 braking system, it can stop so quickly it will leave you breathless. In addition. the modern engine-management electronics allow this car to be driven like a family sedan in today's unavoidably slow traffic. Left: The 1996 Carrera Coupe has the same-size engine as the 1995, but its new "Varioram" induction system raises the peak horsepower slightly to 285. More importantly, the power in the engine's midrange is increased 15 percent, which makes the car even easier to drive normally.

The Boxster—Type 986

The introduction of this new car is said to be a make-or-break event for the Stuttgart factory. The future continues to be uncertain. Will the Boxster, Type 986, save Porsche from a takeover?

The Porsche Boxster styling study was first shown at the Detroit Auto Show in early 1993, and the arrival of the production model has been long awaited, with deposits left at dealerships all around the world. For the first year, demand far exceeded the supply. Powered by a 2.5-liter, 204-horsepower, 4-valve, 6-cylinder water-cooled mid-engine, the Boxster weighs only 2,200 pounds (1,000 kg). This two-seater roadster incorporates the 911 technology. The headlights have polyellipsoid low beams and vari-able focus reflectors for high beams. It has a small trunk in the rear, which leaves room for the mid-engine and for the hidden space that accommodates the convertible top, which disappears into its own storage compartment. The rest of your groceries will have to fit in the front trunk. Behind the seats are two removable travel cases for additional storage. There are rear air intakes behind the door handles that supply air to the engine. Air intakes below the front bumper allow enough air for the radiator, oil cooler, and air-conditioning condenser. Dual airbags and ABS (antilock braking system) are, of course, standard features.

In the center of the dashboard is an LCD screen. Also located on the dashboard are a radio, CD player, TV/video, navigational system, and telephone controls,

Due to its mid-engine design, Porsche's new two-seat roadster for 1997, the Boxster, features two luggage compartments.

Getting Your Porsche's Birth Certificate

Porsche now offers a certificate of authenticity for older models. The original information is retrieved from the original factory kardex specifications at the archives in Ludwigsburg and printed on a certificate useful for restoration and invaluable for resale information. Contact Porsche Cars North America, Inc., Owner Relations Dept., P.O. Box 30911, Reno, NV 89520-3911.

as well as an on-board computer, clock, and space for additional instruments.

The Boxster has rear wheel drive and a five-speed transmission. Seventeen-inch alloy wheels have disc brakes all around; the front discs are ventilated. Porsche plans to introduce a larger, 3.0-liter, 250-horsepower engine in a later version.

The Boxster does have competition in the form of the new BMW Z3 and Mercedes SLK. The Porsche is more powerful; it can outhandle both of these front-engined models and its price falls between the two.

New for 1998

Porsche is always working on new ideas. The next 911, Type 996, is to have a 24-valve flat-6 water-cooled engine based on the Boxster engine and will grow to 300 horsepower.

One of the reasons that the Weissach engineers are moving to a water-cooled engine is racing buffs. This new engine is far more efficient than the version with an air-cooled 2-valve head. Expect to see more Porsches on the track.

The next development, scheduled for 1999, is a 3.3-liter, sequential twin-turbo version of the new flat-6. This power-plant will develop 350 horsepower for the Turbo with a six-speed gearbox. Maybe James Bond will fly in this Porsche Turbo in his next movie.

The 1996 Porsche 911 Turbo is equipped with unique 18-inch aluminum alloy wheels. With the latest ABS 5 braking system, the car can stop sharp from a speed of 62 mph (100kph) in 2.6 seconds!

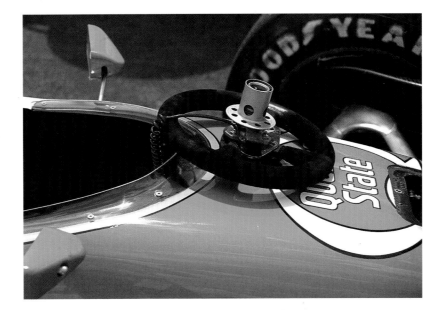

CHAPTER SEVEN

PORSCHE RACING

went to a bullfight a few years ago in Spain. I sat in the front row and could see into the eyes of the bullfighter, not to mention the eyes of the bull. But it was the eyes of the bullfighter that most intrigued me.

I have been to many automobile races and have photographed the drivers from the pit area and track, shooting right into the cockpit, looking right into their faces. It fascinated me to see that the eyes of the bullfighter was the same as those of the race car drivers.

Does that mean anything? It could be that both are the type of person who enjoys getting close to danger and excitement. They know their limits and love every minute of what they are doing and wouldn't change it for the world.

EARLY RACING
550/550A, RSK, RS60/RS61

The racing cars that Porsche develops are designed to sell cars. The factory spends money to make money. Many of the successful advanced developments made through the years for the track automobiles turned up on the street models the following year. Racing provided a quick way for the technical department to test an idea after it passed the safety development. Porsche always believed that racing was the only true test of a car's value. One twenty-four-hour race was as good a test as two to three years in the hands of an average driver on the street.

In the early 1950s, when the Porsche was first manufactured and exported to North America, the "gentleman racer" considered the car for road racing. The 356 was first thought of as a good rally vehicle and later was taken to track events, where it easily beat the MGs and Simcas in the small bore class (under 1,500cc). In Europe, however, where racing was taken more seriously, it was a different matter. High-performance small sports racers

flew by the Porsches in sprint events and the only saving grace was a long-distance race. Porsche won rallies in 1950 with the 1.1-liter 356.

That same year, Walter Glöckler, produced a sports-racing car with Porsche components, a 1.1-liter Porsche engine, and VW running gear. It was a single-seater open car with the driver placed almost in the center, similar to past designs of early race cars that Porsche had been involved with, such as the Cisitalia. That first year, the car won the under-1,100cc sports-car class in Germany.

Starting in 1951, Porsche made an agreement with Glöckler to produce a sports-racing car using the Porsche name in exchange for the use of the latest engine technology. The cars became known as the Glöckler-Porsches. Changes were made on each car built, such as increasing the size of the interior and adding headlights—one even had a removable roof. This was the beginning of a history of winning races within Europe and, by late 1951, in North America as well. This racer—now with a 1.5-liter engine and weighing only 990 pounds (446 kg)—broke many records, from short sprints to long-distance endurance events. The name "Porsche" was now recorded and mentioned in newspapers, which was the free advertising that Porsche needed.

In 1951 and 1952, Porsche's aluminum-bodied coupes with the 1.1-liter engine (1,100cc) won their class at the 24-hour race at Le Mans, France. By 1952, a lightweight America Roadster was offered to the North American racer through the New York importer Max Hoffman with delivery for the following year (see page 24). Other than this small effort, Porsche did not feel ready to produce a true race car for its buyers. The following year, the English-language sales brochures (printed in Germany) listed the 1952 racing results from Italy, France, Holland, Austria, Germany, Portugal, Sweden, and the United States. Besides winning the Italian Championship for 1,500cc Gran Turismo, Porsche had also won the German

Teo Fabi at the wheel of the Foster's March–Porsche Indy car.

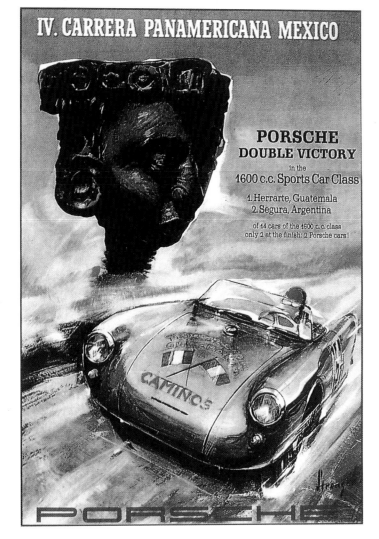

Championship in both the 1,100cc and 1,500cc categories, as well as other first, second, and third place wins. These events were not won by race cars, but with street cars prepared for track events. In many cases, the cars actually driven to and from the event and not trailered.

Two Type 550 Porsches were commissioned to be built by Glöckler for 1953. Both cars (serial numbers 550-01 and 550-02) would have the 1500 Super engine and removable hardtop. In their early races the cars finished high in their 1,500cc class, including first place for the 550-01 at Nurburgring. Both cars won numerous events in Europe, including hill climbs, and even went on to the Carrera Panamericana races—one winning its class and

the other car retiring early. The only other Porsche to finish in this class was a stock Porsche 356.

This was the start of the true racing Porsches from Zuffenhausen. Under the direction of Ernst Fuhrmann, who years later became the president of Porsche, a new four-cam, air-cooled engine was developed. (Earlier engines had been in the pushrod configuration.) This new engine design became one of the most successful developments in motor racing. The car was a full-fledged competition racer and was shown at the Paris Salon in 1953, with production racing Porsches not seen until 1954. The limited production run of the Type 550 also became known as the Spyder or 550 Spyder. The price

Top: *A beautifully restored Porsche 550 Spyder. Although it was not meant to be used, the convertible top was required for European endurance racers. Bottom: The cockpit of a Type 550. The painted tubes of the frame can be seen at the sides and bottom. Typical of a race car, there are just enough gauges and controls to get the job done.*

for a light aluminum alloy Spyder in 1955 was about twice the price of a standard street Porsche. The RS designation translates to *Rennsport*, or "racing sports." About one hundred units were produced before the updated 550A/1500RS was seen in 1956.

Racing provided the attention and publicity necessary for Porsche to sell its street cars. As their racing successes continued, sales followed. Porsche always raced in Europe in any competition available, but it never officially raced in North America in those early days. One reason was the financial obligation, and the other was the distance from the factory in Germany. Fortunately, a group of amateur and semiprofessional drivers brought

Top left: *James Dean sitting on the door of his 1955 Speedster.* **Bottom right:** *James Dean before leaving for the Salinas sports races on September 30, 1955, in his 550 Spyder.*

The Legend of James Dean

James Dean was a quiet, reserved man. At only twenty-four years old, he was achieving greater and greater success in the acting world. At the time of his death on September 30, 1955, he was filming the movie *Giant* with Rock Hudson and Elizabeth Taylor.

Dean's street car was a Porsche Speedster, but he wanted to go even faster than that machine would take him. In 1955, like today, the police were not too happy to see anyone racing on the street, so the next best place to go fast was on a race track; the best fast car was a Porsche 550 Spyder. Dean made a deal with the local dealer, John von Newmann's Competition Motors in Hollywood, California, whereby he would turn in his Speedster and pay an additional $3,000

for the new 550. When the car arrived in early September, there was not much time before an upcoming sports car race in Salinas, California, so Dean drove the car around the Hollywood hills to accumulate mileage.

As the race day approached, Dean felt he needed more break-in mileage on the engine before redlining it on the track, so he chose to drive to the event, inviting along his mechanic, Rolf Wuetherich. But tragedy occurred at dusk on Route 466 near the community of Cholame: Dean's 550 collided with another vehicle at an intersection. His mechanic, though severely injured, lived, but only the legend of James Dean survives today.

Dean's Porsche 550 Spyder:
Shipped from Germany: July 15, 1955
Chassis No.: 550-0055
Engine No.: 90 059
Transmission No.: 10 146

Porsche 550 Spyders:
Facts: 75 customer cars were built
Chassis Numbers: 0016 to 0090
Today: Porsche 550 Spyders can be seen in historic races and some automotive museums

their own Porsches out to the tracks and raced with great success.

Besides winning races in Europe, Porsches began to turn up at events in the Bahamas, Guatemala, Brazil, and Mexico, as well as the United States, campaigned by private entrants. In early 1956, the Carrera, Porsche's new coupe, started racing in the United States. The 1957 sales literature stated that "the new Porsche series was proudly named for the Mexican road classic" (in reference to the Carrera Panamericana). The Carrera prototypes won first place in their class starting in 1954 and placed third overall.

By 1957, the 356A Carrera Speedsters with the GT (Grand Touring) engine in the 1,600cc class were the big winners. One of the most famous sports drivers of the day was Bruce Jennings in the four-cam Carrera GT Speedster, of which he owned three. The cars were all painted the same, ruby red with a silver nose, but with different suspension and gearing for particular courses—one for a short course, one medium, and one long. Bruce won more races with a Porsche from 1959 to 1969 than anyone in the world.

Porsche had some success with Formula II in Europe in 1957 and 1960. Privateers bought cars, rebuilt them, and at times even beat the factory teams. Each year the total number of Porsches seen in the winner's circle increased. By 1958 the 550 RS and the RSK were included, and the Carrera was collecting wins on both continents. In 1959, first (RSK), second (RS), third (Carrera), and fourth (Carrera) place awards were won at the Targa Florio. The next year an RS60 won.

The RS60 and RS61 were both built on a similar Type 718 chassis, the reason why you may sometimes see the car named after this chassis, such as 718-1500RS or 718-RS 60.

By 1962, the RS Porsches were no longer competitive in the racing world, and during 1963 Porsche was working on the development of a new sports-racing car: the 904. Meanwhile, the chassis of the British car-maker, Elva,

Left: *A well-preserved Carrera GT Speedster. This car was extensively and successfully campaigned in the 1960s by Bruce Jennings.* Below: *This 1958 Porsche RSK Spyder has spent most of its life running Pennsylvania Hillclimb Association events.*

was combined with the Porsche engine to make an Elva-Porsche. These cars raced at the end of 1963 successfully and continued into 1964. Even today, it is not uncommon to find a Porsche engine combined with another manufacturer's chassis in a winning combination.

RACING THEN
Carrera GTS/904, 906, 907, 908, 909, and 910

Unveiled in November 1963 and officially known as the Carerra GTS, this fantastic Porsche rapidly became known as the 904; today it is rare for the Carrera designation to be used. A production run of one hundred cars was planned, with the first car delivered in 1964, but it appears that the factory delivered about 10 percent more cars to its customers. The factory offered this race car to the buyer as an out-of-the-box buy-and-drive deal. The body was made of fiberglass and bonded directly to the frame. The 904s were originally designed to have a 2.0-liter, 6-cylinder, air-cooled engine mounted in front of the rear axle, with a 5-speed gearbox, but development problems with this new 6-cylinder caused Porsche to resurrect the reliable 4-cylinder Carrera engine. A few later factory racing versions possessed 6- and even 8-cylinder engines. The Carrera GTS was considered one of the most outstanding models in the history of early Porsches.

The factory considered building an additional one hundred cars but decided against it because the next-generation racing model, the 906, was nearing completion. Officially called the Carrera 6, fifty identical cars with 6-cylinder engines (the racing version of the same engine that was designed for the latest street 911) were completed for the 1966 season to race in the Sports Car production class. A few other 906s were produced with various modifications, such as a 2.0-liter, 8-cylinder

Type 904: The Carrera GTS

Officially known as the Carrera GTS, this fantastic Porsche soon became known everywhere as the 904. The production run was planned for one hundred, with a second group of one hundred to be started when the first group was completed in April 1964. But the factory decided not to continue with the next group of 904s and to concentrate its efforts on the 906. (It is believed that as many as 10 percent more of the 904s were built using 6- and 8-cylinder engines, though no one is sure when these were produced.)

The early sales literature for the car was printed in German, but that did not stop the North American market from buying most of the cars. The Americans were excited about racing and wanted anything that Porsche could give them. Like the Spyder, RS, and RSK, this GTS was intended for sports competition; the brochure explained that "the purchaser is handed an impact-ready sports instrument." The 904 was also designed to be used on the street, was easy to drive, and even had a windshield wiper, but it contained very little room for a passenger, who had to rest his or her feet on a 12 volt battery. But by race-car standards, the accommodations were very luxurious.

The 904's 2.0-liter engine was directly behind the driver, with 185 horsepower at 7,000 rpm; it was an uprated four-cam Carrera. The rear bodywork could be rotated away from the cabin or could be removed as a unit. This was the first time that Porsche had used a fiberglass body, and it was bonded to the chassis, which was only $41^1/2$ inches (105cm) from the ground and weighed only 1,350 pounds (613 kg) with no fuel in the 29-gallon (110-liter) tank. The top speed was 150 mph (241 kph), and it could go from 0 to 60 mph (96.5 kph) in 6.4 seconds and from 50 to 70 mph (80 to 113 kph) in 2.5 seconds—quite impressive for 1964.

The racing rules for manufacturing a car for the GT class were unusual: the passenger compartment had to be completely furnished, the car had to have a full set of instruments, and the standard equipment, such as a spare tire, battery, and the large gas tank, all had to be fitted. Luggage space was also required, but since the size only had to be 65×40×20 cm, you were alright if you didn't mind putting your clothes in a box. There were many more requirements, but the major rule was that at least one hundred identical examples had to have been built.

This car was designed to win. Today you may see a 904 at a vintage race, but more than likely one will show up at a car show. It is hard to believe this modern-looking car was designed and built in the 1960s. It is perhaps the most unique Porsche that Porsche ever built.

Opposite page: *Initially named the Carrera GTS, the Porsche Type 904 race car is known by its number.* Left: *The Porsche Type 904 race car went from an idea to the prototype stage in only eight months. The fiberglass body is glued to the box-member frame, a concept that was patented. The air scoops cool the rear brakes. Fully race-prepared, it weighed 1,410 pounds (635 kg).*

A restored Porsche Carrera 6, also known as a 906. These cars were offered for sale in early 1966 and were about fifty percent more expensive than the cost of a 904 less than two years earlier. With a fiberglass body and a tubular space frame, it weighed less than 1,400 pounds (630 kg).

engine or fuel injection added to the six, that ended up racing in the prototype classification. The 906s finished successfully in races on both sides of the Atlantic Ocean, raced by the factory and by private entrants.

The man behind the racing department and the 906, the head of Porsche research and development, was Dr. Ferdinand Piëch, Dr. Ferry Porsche's nephew. The next big project to come out of Porsche was the 910, designed to be a factory prototype car not sold to private owners through 1967. Also during this time, the homologation rules changed for the Sports Car division, requiring only twenty-five cars to be manufactured. The 910 automatically became eligible at the beginning of 1968.

The 907, a similar car except for its shape and right-hand drive, was under development at the same time as the 910, but it was not introduced until several months after. These cars, as well as the 909, were heavily raced in European hill climbs. The factory was always experi-

menting with gearbox changes, different suspensions, and lighter metals. A new 3.0-liter, 8-cylinder racing engine was developed for the 908 long-tail for endurance races and raced from 1968 through the mid-1970s.

Race fever had taken over the Porsche racing branch. The models 907, 908, 909, and 910 (Bergspyders) were developed at breakneck speeds and taken off to race by the factory racing team as soon as they were completed. Engines were designed with both 6 and 8 cylinders.

The 917, 917K, 917L, 917PA, 917/10, and 917/30

As discussed earlier, the official rules to homologate a car for racing required twenty-five vehicles to be built in one year. Though assembly of one engine for the 917 coupe took a total of 160 man-hours, the Porsche factory met the homologation requirement in 363 days.

The 917K was the short-tailed version designed for slower tracks. The 917L, tested for high-speed long straights, was 2 feet (60 cm) longer but had handling problems in poor weather.

The first overall win for Porsche at the famous 24-Hours of Le Mans was in 1970 in a 917 (short-tail version); second went to a 917L; and third to a 908. Although Porsche had won in its class before, it had never before won the first-place overall trophy. It was a great triumph for the year that included the 24-Hours of Daytona (first and second), Brands Hatch (first, second, and third), Monza 1000 kms (first), Nürburgring and Targa Florio (first and second with 908s), Watkins Glen 6-Hours (first and second), and the Osterreichring (first). In three years of competition, from 1969 to 1971, the 917K won fifteen of the twenty-four World Championship races.

Volkswagen of America negotiated a special contract with Porsche AG to flagship a car for the Can-Am series (Canadian-American Challenge Cup Championship) that would use the name Porsche+Audi, the marketing company for the Porsche in the United States. The car was designed and built from a 917 coupe, with its top cut off, and used the designation 917PA for Porsche+Audi. The 917PA was never a very successful racer in 1969, and Porsche did not race in the series in 1970.

In mid-March 1969, Porsche introduced the new Type 917 race car at the Geneva Auto Show (this is the cover of the sales brochure). It debuted with a 4.5-liter, flat-12, 520-horsepower engine and weighed 2,050 pounds (923 kg) with fuel. Twenty cars were offered for sale.

Top: A restored 917 at a vintage car race at Watkins Glen, New York, in autumn 1979. Bottom: Mark Donohue on his way to winning the 1973 Can-Am Championship in a 917/30, most likely the most powerful circuit racer ever built. Its turbocharged 5.4-liter, flat-12 engine developed 1,100 horsepower.

In 1971, the 917 ran in 5.0-liter form in the Can-Am series as a 917, and by 1972 it was turbocharged for the series, winning six out of eight races. The championship was taken by George Follmer driving the refined 917/10. This car led to the evolution of the 917/30, driven by Mark Donohue, who went on to win the 1973 Can-Am Championship. The 917 won a total of eight of eight races with Donohue, who came in first place in six. The car was removed from racing due to regulation changes by 1975, but not before it made a closed course record at Talladega in Alabama in a 221.12-mph (355.85-kph) run driven by Donohue.

Carrera RSR, 935, and 936

Porsche developed the RS and RSR in late 1972. These cars looked like the 911 but with unusually large front air dams and protruding rear ducktails designed to provide the needed downforce to stabilize the car on the track.

Two years later, the engine was turbocharged, and the rear had a more extreme whale tail. (Much of the turbocharging experience had been obtained from the 917s.) The 911-based Carrera RSRs were used as the development base for the 934s and 935s to come.

When the new 1976 regulations for the Group 5 World Championship of Makes were announced, Porsche decided to use the 930 Turbo as a base. The number designation 935 was picked. The rules allowed a "free" design of the front fenders, so the 911 look was replaced with a sloping hood with louvers above the front wheels. This look became a trademark of the 935 and became so popular that the Porsche factory offered a 935-type front-end option on a street 911SC.

The rear of the race car was a built-up standard Turbo spoiler, as required by the rules, with an adjustable rear edge. All rustproofing was removed and anything that would lighten the car was taken off. The front windshield

A 1974 Turbo Carrera race car. Its turbocharged 2.14-liter engine developed 490 horsepower. Handling improvements made on this car were later used in the 911 Turbo street cars.

Top: Daytona 24-Hour, 1983. Porsche 935 No. 5, driven by Bob Akin, Dale Whittington, and John O'Steen, leads 935 No. 86, driven by Bruce Leven, Hurley Haywood, and Al Holbert, into the hairpin. Bottom: An air hose connected to this 935 race car operates the on-board air jacks to raise the car.

was safety glass, but every other body piece was plastic. Anything that wasn't plastic was aluminum or titanium, and there was just one seat for the driver.

The racing awards earned by the 935 were numerous, including the World Championship of Makes and Sports Car World Championship and an overall win at Le Mans in 1979. The 935 continued to win high honors through 1982, with factory-sponsored cars as well as privateers winning thirteen victories that year.

The FIA organization (Federation Internationale de l'Automobile), in charge or worldwide racing, had been working on new regulations for the Group 6 sports racing class. These new regulations for racing took effect in 1976, and in that year both Group 5 and Group 6 raced

together. The Porsche factory had been working on a new secret project that turned out to be the 936. Even though the number designation was close, it did not look anything like the 935. With the new regulations coming into effect at this time, the 935 and the 936 ran together that year, with Porsche winning a double championship in both Group 5 and Group 6, adding another award-winning record for Porsche.

The time it took Porsche to develop the 936 was short. The parts were taken from existing proven race cars. The engine was from the 911 RSR Turbo Carrera; the chassis, transmission, and running gear were from the 917/30 Can-Am Spyder. The body design was a cross between the 917/10 Spyder and the 908 Spyder and had an aluminum space frame.

The 936 did not win its first race in 1976, but that was practically the only time. The 936 went on to win the 24-Hours of Le Mans, the World Sports Car, and Group 6 World Makes awards. By 1977, Porsche decided to cut back its factory racing teams and only ran in the Le Mans race, where the 936 took the win again. A private entry in a 935 won Le Mans in 1979. The Porsche factory did not see the winner's circle at Le Mans again until 1981, this time with the 2.65-liter engine that had been developed for the Indianapolis 500 car that never ran, in the body of a 936, and with the four-speed transmission from the 917 Turbo Can-Am car. One of the drivers was Jacky Ickx, who celebrated his fifth win at Le Mans. It was the thirtieth year that Porsche had been involved with the French endurance race and also its fiftieth year as a company.

The Racing 924

In 1980, the 924 was racing in the SCCA (Sports Car Club of America) races across the United States, winning the SCCA D Production. By 1981, a new World Endurance

A 1977 Porsche 936 race car. This car underwent extensive but subtle changes from the 1976 version to reduce the aerodynamic drag. Power output from the 2.14-liter turbocharged 6-cylinder, taken from the 1974 Turbo Carrera, was about 525 Horsepower. The car weighed just over 1,600 pounds (720 kg).

Top and bottom: *Details from a 1977 Porsche 936. Opposite page: At the Porsche test track near the town of Weissach, the 956s duplicate their 1-2-3 win at the 1982 Le Mans 24-Hour race.*

Championship began. The 924 Carrera GT, based on the 924 Turbo, with a 4-cylinder, 2.0-liter engine with a turbocharger, was eligible to enter the endurance challenge (referred to as a GTR). Porsche entered three race-prepared cars in the Le Mans race that year, finishing sixth, twelfth, and thirteenth. The street version known as the Carrera GT, with a production run of four hundred cars, was sold out immediately. The Carrera GTS production run was only fifty cars, designed with racing equipment, and all were street legal in Germany.

The 956 and 962

Racing in North America in 1982 was centered around Porsche 935s in the SCCA Trans-Am and IMSA (International Motor Sports Association) Camel GT circuits. Porsche also wanted to enter the new Group C long-distance races. The rules allowed freedom of design, but each car had to meet a mileage restriction; the car had to be quick and fuel-efficient. The car designed by the engineers was the prototype 956. Not only did this new car have an undefeated season, it won Le Mans in a one-two-three sweep.

The 956, and its successor, the 962C, won six straight Le Mans races from 1982 through 1987. The 956 used a twin-turbo, twin ignition, water-cooled head from the 935 flat-six and evolved into a complete water-cooled engine. It started with a 2.6-liter engine and progressed to a 2.8-liter, 3.0-liter, and finally the 3.2-liter of today.

The 962 Retires

In 1984, the Porsche factory redesigned its 956 Group C Turbo Coupe to meet the latest IMSA Camel GT safety regulations to race in North America. For the car to race in the GTP division, the chassis had to be changed so that the driver's feet were located behind the front axle line.

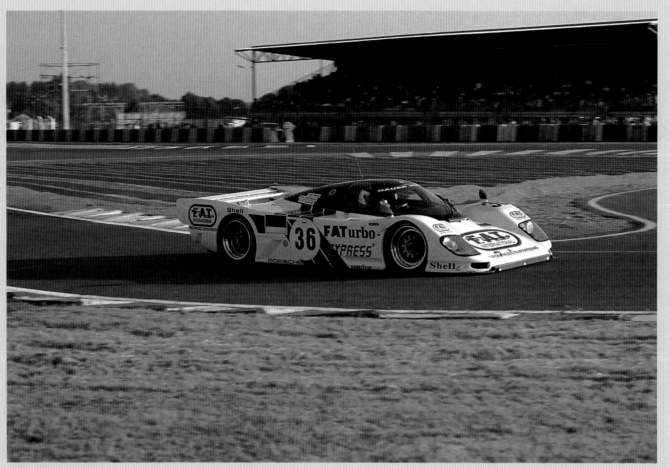

Hurley Haywood

Above: *Hurley Haywood is the winner of ten Endurance Classics, more than anyone else in racing history. And he won all ten in Porsches!*
Right: *In 1994, Hurley Haywood, Yannick Dalmas, and Mauro Baldi won the 24-Hours of Le Mans in this 962LM. It was the final victory for the 962 model, as changes in the rules forced this most successful Porsche to be retired from competition.*

Hurley Haywood bought his first Porsche and started racing sports cars when he was in college, more than 25 years ago. After an afternoon of practice on the track, Hurley was driving faster than his teacher. He now has a total of 10 wins at Endurance Classics, more than anyone else in Racing history. The races include five Daytona (Florida) 24-Hour, two Sebring (Florida) 12-Hour, and three Le Mans (France) 24-Hour victories. He is two-time IMSA GT Champion, 1988 SCCA TransAm Champion, 1991 Supercar Champion, 1992 Runner-up Supercar Champion,

four-time Norelco Cup winner, top active IMSA point leader, fastest Indy Rookie for 1981 (with 18 Indy Car starts), 1994 North American GT Endurance Champion—and he is still active in racing today. He was the first driver to win the 24-Hours of Daytona and the 24-Hours of Le Mans in the same year and went on to repeat these wins a second year.

Hurley says the keys to his success are driving fast enough to win and not making mistakes. These two things, along with preserving your race car, are what win these very tough tests of man and machine.

Racing will always be part of Hurley's life, whether in the form of endurance events, short sprints, or even vintage races, where he can drive cars that he raced in the 1970s.

At the Daytona 24-Hour in 1989, the Porsche 962 No. 67 (chassis no. 962 108B), with drivers Derek Bell, John Andretti, and Bob Wollek, came in first overall. Following page: A side view of this car.

The engine was also revised to a 2.8-liter, air-cooled, single-turbo, single-ignition, 934-based power plant. The new car was known as the 962 and also had design changes, such as an upgraded ignition and increased engine size. It continued to compete and chalk up wins through 1994 with a 962LM at the 24-Hours of Le Mans. It was to be the last race for the 962 model, as changes in the rules forced this most successful Porsche to be retired from competition.

Production-Based Racing

In the 1990s, international sports car racing has seen the return of race cars based on production cars. Porsche 911-based cars scored overall victories in 1993 in the grueling 24-hour races at Spa, Belgium, and the famed Nurburgring in Germany. In the United States, Porsche 911 Turbos won three consecutive IMSA Bridgestone Supercar Championships (1991, 1992, and 1993), a record-breaking fifteen Supercar race victories.

The SCCA World Challenge Manufacturers Championship was won by Porsche in 1994 and 1995. Porsche drivers and teams captured six 1995 North American road racing championships. The IMSA Exxon GTS-2 Driver's Championship was awarded to Jorge Trejos after his second victory with his 911 RSR 3.8 Porsche. David Murry drove his 911 GT2 to win the SCCA World Challenge Sports Class Drivers Championship and went on to drive with teammate Jochen Rohr, earning Porsche's second straight World Challenge Sports Class Manufacturers Championship. These same two Porsche drivers went on to win the over-

Below: The drivers Joe Cogbill, Charles Slater, and Bill Auberlen soldiered on through two Florida downpours to win the GTS-2 class at the rain-shortened 12-Hours of Sebring in 1995. Opposite page: The Footwork Porsche at the start of the 1991 Formula 1 season in Phoenix, Arizona.

all score for the One Lap of America contest, driving 4,100 miles (6,597 km) at the controls of a 1996 Porsche 911 Turbo. A similar car, driven by Jeff Zwart, won the famed Pikes Peak Hillclimb in the High Performance Showroom Stock Class (see page 131).

The Canadian Valvoline Touring Car Championship for 1995 was won by Rick Bye and Harry Hatch in a Porsche 968. At the same time, Canadian Stephane Veilleux drove a Porsche 968 to the Grand Sports Drivers Championship in the Canadian Magna Enduro Series.

Porsche has won more overall victories than any other manufacturer between 1960 and 1995. The list is overwhelming.

13 Overall LeMans 24-Hour Victories
19 Overall Daytona 24-Hour Victories
17 Overall Sebring 12-Hour Victories
11 Overall Targa Florio Victories
13 World Manufacturers Team Championships
27 IMSA Camel GT Manufacturers Championships
37 IMSA Firehawk Race Victories
15 IMSA Supercar Race Victories
3 IMSA Supercar Manufacturers Championships
286 IMSA Camel GT Race/Class Victories

Racing into the Future

Porsche will return to Le Mans with a mid-engine GT car that, visually, is based on the 911. The engine will be a turbocharged $3\frac{1}{2}$-liter version of the water-cooled flat-6 that, at this writing, is slated for future production. The chassis of this new racer will reputedly serve as the basis for the redesigned and mid-engine 911 due out in the late 1990s.

RACING THEN AND NOW

It was relatively easy to participate in amateur racing in the 1950s and 1960s, but as the drivers and manufacturers became more professional, so did the racing governing bodies. Today's cars are classified in many different categories and even look-alike cars in the same race can be in different divisions.

When Porsche goes racing, Porsche expects to win. The company spends extensive amounts of money, and the Porsche engineering department is dedicated to the project full-time. Porsche chose to enter the Formula 1 arena at the start of the 1961 season. By late 1962, its new 8-cylinder, air-cooled power plant had won two victories in the hands of Dan Gurney. But the Porsche fac-

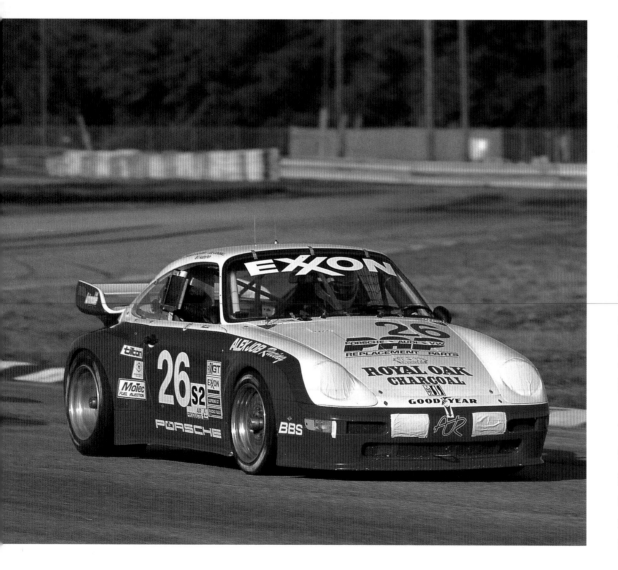

In 1992, Porsche won four of seven races in the new IMSA Bridgestone Supercar Championship for street exotics, which gave Porsche enough points to win the Manufacturers Championship. Hurley Haywood became the first recipient of the Drivers Championship. The Brumos 911 Turbos, co-driven by Haywood and Hans Stuck, revived the classic paint scheme of the Brumos Porsches of the early 1970s.

The cars in the series, designated Supercars, included other exotics such as the Lotus Esprit Turbo, Dodge Stealth Turbo, Consulier, and the Corvette L-98. To equalize the competition a handicap was added: the more powerful the car, the more weight they were required to carry. All were lightly modified street stock high-performance cars and competed on Bridgestone Potenza street radial tires in short 30-minute sprint races.

tory made the decision to continue with sports car racing and not to continue with Formula 1 at that time.

Porsche was not seen in the Formula 1 program again until 1983, when the development department designed and built an engine commissioned in 1981 for the TAG company. It was a twin-turbo, 1.5-liter, V-6 engine for the McLaren chassis and made its debut at the Dutch Grand Prix. The cars were driven by Niki Lauda and Alain Prost. Porsche continued with the team from 1983 to 1987, earning twenty-five race victories, two World Manufacturers Championships, and three World Drivers Championships for Team McLaren.

Porsche returned to Formula 1 in the 1990s. The official name for the new race car was the Footwork Porsche FA12. The new engine was a 3.5-liter, nonturbocharged motor built by Porsche for Footwork Arrows Racing, Ltd., of Milton Keynes, England. Footwork, Ltd. is a diversified Japanese-based company involved in food, hotels, insur-

ance, and transportation. Testing programs resulted in the all-new V-12 engine incorporated into a new chassis, with a six-speed transverse gearbox, rear suspension, electrical system, radiators, undertray, fuel system, redesigned dash and seat bulkhead, and a more efficient cooling system. Other features included four overhead camshafts with four valves per cylinder, aluminum alloy cylinder heads and crankcase top, magnesium alloy crankcase bottom, and titanium connecting rods. The Porsche engine was first tested on the Footwork Arrows A 11C chassis. The Footwork Porsche, with its new engine, chassis, and body, was introduced in April 1991 at the San Marino Grand Prix. But sadly, the car did not perform very well. It was jointly decided, close to mid-season, to pull the Porsche engine for more development, but it was never reentered. The Footwork car continued to be raced with a Cosworth engine for the full season. Porsche has decided to devote its time to other racing ventures.

The Firehawk Season

In the IMSA Firestone Firehawk Endurance Championship, Porsche races in the Grand Sports category for street stock automobiles. The 944 S2 had an outstanding 1990 year that continued into 1991. A few recognizable names of the drivers are Bobby Akin (the son of Bob Akin of 956 fame), Fred Baker (SCCA Showroom Stock GT National Champion), and Bruce Jenner (Olympic decathalon gold medal winner). Porsche was the winner in the Grand Sports Manufacturers Championship in 1985, 1991, 1992, and 1994, the first time in the history of the series that any one model has won a total of 37 races in the Premier Grand Sports category.

The Indianapolis Challenge

The reason behind European sports car manufacturers wanting to race in North America rests fundamentally with the publicity that racing generates. Racing simply helps to sell more cars. The Indy 500 is the largest single sporting event in the world. Even on practice days, the fans in attendance at the Indy outnumber the fans watching a typical football game.

Porsche's participation at Indy goes back to 1979, when Porsche unveiled a car to race the following year. Danny Ongais was to drive an Interscope Team car with a Porsche turbocharged 2.6-liter, flat-six engine with water-cooled heads, which evolved from the 935 and 936. Although the car was fully developed and built, it never ran.

Porsche designed an engine and chassis for a development car that made its debut in the fall of 1987, but after extensive testing, Porsche decided on the chassis built by the March company for 1988. This was the first year that a Porsche-powered car had qualified for the Indianapolis 500.

In 1989, Porsche had a great year racing in the CART/PPG (Champion Auto Racing Team/Pittsburgh Plate Glass) Indy Car World Series circuit. The start of the season was slow, but by the end of the year, with Teo Fabi driving, Porsche had received points for ten straight races including two pole positions and finished fourth in the series for the season. By 1990, the Porsche engine was increased, with more power in the top end and a more sensitive throttle response. With the chassis already under construction, March suffered a setback when the governing bodies voted not to allow a carbon fiber chassis, sending production back to square one and leaving little time to test the car before the first race. In addition, a decision was made to race two cars, using Teo Fabi in one and John Andretti in the other, so two cars had to be constructed. The March 90P chassis was given a 2.65-liter Porsche V-8 Indy engine.

A window sticker and jacket patch made for Porsche's intended 1980 Indy venture.

Right: *John Andretti in car*
No. 41, the Foster's March–
Porsche, during a pit stop
at the Indy 500 in 1990.
Bottom: *Teo Fabi drives the*
Quaker State Porsche Indy
car during the wet 1989
Meadowlands Grand Prix
in New Jersey.

The 1990 season was not very promising. Overall, the three-year Indy Program produced Porsche's first Indy Car victory and three pole positions with twenty-nine top-10 finishes. Porsche has not raced since 1990, and there are no guarantees for the future.

One of the original Indy cars, Foster's Quaker State Porsche, can now be seen at the Indianapolis Motor Speedway Hall of Fame Museum as an example of one of the most modern race cars that competed in the 500-mile (800-km) race. The "Foster's" part of the name derives from the Australian brewing company, a sponsor of the British Grand Prix and the Foster's Formula 1 Australian Grand Prix in November, the final race at the end of the Formula 1 season. Beginning in 1996, though, Australia will become the very first race of the season.

RALLYING

Real racing is said to be the rally. Most endurance rally racing lasts days, through demanding terrain. In 1968, Vic Elford drove a 911 in the prestigious Monte Carlo Rally to a first-place win, the first overall victory for Porsche. Within the same month, Elford also won the 24-Hours of Daytona in a 907, the first overall victory for Porsche in a 24-hour race. His spectacular record has never been duplicated by another driver.

The most exotic event was the Paris to Dakar rally. (Dakar is located in Senegal, on the west coast of Africa.) Most of the two-week rally took place in the Sahara Desert. Porsche participated in 1984 with 92 other entrants; it entered three cars, coming in first, sixth, and twenty-sixth place. The Porsches entered were four-wheel-drive Carrera 911s. In 1986 Porsche entered the rally again, this time with the new 959 in rally trim, and won the race again. Porsche has not engaged in any official factory-sponsored rallying since 1986.

OTHER PORSCHE RACING
Amateur Racing

The SCCA has races almost every weekend throughout the United States during the spring and summer months, ending with a final week-long national championship event in October at Mid-Ohio Sports Car Course, near Lexington, Ohio. These races, both for regional and national points, are designed for the fun of racing. The drivers are amateur racers, some of whom are hoping for the big break into professional racing; others have been racing for more than thirty years. Actor Paul Newman raced in these events throughout North America, including his home state of Connecticut.

Hotline

For the latest North American Porsche racing news, you can call the Porsche Motorsport telephone hotline at (702) 348-3962.

Off-Road Racing

Porsche power is found in many places, including the mountain known as Pike's Peak. In 1994 rallyist Jeff Zwart won the Pike's Peak Open Class in a specially prepared turbocharged Carrera 4, and in 1995, driving a 1996 Porsche 911 Turbo, he won the High Performance Showroom Stock category, finishing 11 seconds faster than his closest competitor. For the first time in the 73-year history of the Colorado-based event, snow and icy road conditions forced organizers to end the race at the

A 1996 Porsche 911 Turbo on its way to winning its class at the Pike's Peak, Colorado, hill climb in July 1995. The Turbo's all-wheel drive and the BFGoodrich R1 tires were certainly instrumental in this victory. The driver, Jeff Zwart, completed the 8.63-mile course 11 seconds faster than his closest competitor.

12,786-foot (3,897 m) mark, 3.78 miles (6 km) short of the 14,110-foot (4,300 m) summit.

VINTAGE AND HISTORIC RACING

Anyone can go to a race, even a race that features vintage and historic racing cars, and almost anyone can race one of these cars—even on a limited budget. There are more than 200 vintage events a year in North America alone, and when you add in the United Kingdom, all of Europe, and the "down under" groups, the count continues to multiply. Each group has its own rules for classifying an eligible vehicle, so to become a participant you will have to do some investigating; if you

This restored single-seat race car was originally a Porsche RSK Spyder, which was purchased new in 1958 by Grand Prix driver Jean Behra. The chassis was immediately reworked and fitted with this special body. It was used in 1500cc Formula II races in 1959 and into 1960. The engine remained the reliable 4-cam.

are a first-time racing enthusiast, you can, at least, get a sense of the basic requirements. If you look back at the early racing part of this chapter, you will be surprised to find that many of these cars are now racing in vintage and historic events.

Vintage and historic racing is a sport; it is not professional racing. There are at least two types of vintage racers: drivers who want only to take their cars on the track and bring them up to speed; and those who want to go to the edge, the max, of both car and driver.

Vintage and historic racing is part social and part competitive. This type of racing is designed for the friendly. The cars are carefully prepared for safety and the attitude of the driver should be the same. There definitely is wheel-to-wheel competition, but the main purpose is to have fun. Drivers do not want to hurt their vehicles or themselves.

The differences between vintage and historic can get complicated, with the size of the engine determining what group the car will be racing in. Some clubs may classify cars in different ways, but basically pre-war, post-war, production cars, and sports racers built before 1963 are in the vintage category. There is a separate classification that includes all Formula cars (Junior, Vee, Formula I, II, and III, and Formula Ford) built before 1969. Some associations classify these cars through 1963. The historic class includes production cars and prototype and race cars built between 1960 and 1973, with some overlap depending on the size of the engine. The only way to really tell what car is in what class is to buy a program at the event you are attending. The cars will be classified for each race.

There is a general conduct "13/13" rule that drivers are subject to: if you are at fault in an incident that causes damage to your car or anyone else's car, you are out of that event and on probation for thirteen months. Any further incidents while on probation will result in sus-

Left: *The 1967 911R was a lightweight 911 (1,810 pounds [815 kg], dry) with a slightly modified 210-horse-power Carrera 6 engine. The fenders, bumpers, doors, and lids were fiberglass. Only twenty-three of these were built; plans for a run of five hundred were abandoned due to the economy of that time. Following page: A 1966 Porsche Carrera 6, also known as a 906, next to a 1967 Porsche 910 (right). It is very difficult to distinguish between these two models. This photograph illustrates some key points where they differ: the shape of the headlight covers, the air scoops, and the center-lock wheels, which debuted on the 910.*

The Concours d'Elegance

con-cours (kon-koor´) n. French. 1. moving together; gathering. 2. competition.
el-e-gance (el´e-gans) n. French. 1. the quality of being elegant. 2. anything elegant.

The above definitions could describe the Concours d'Elegance events, which began when automobiles were first being exhibited in Europe prior to World War I. These exhibits were displays of objects of art rather than performance events. In the early days both the occupants and the machine were on display and judged as a complete package. Today only the automobile is judged.

The judging is based on the best preparation, restoration, maintenance, and originality of the cars. Each organization conducting an event will have its own rules. The automobiles are divided into categories: by age, sometimes by marque, and by a classification that could include the quantity built. Depending on the total number of entrants, the designated categories are then broke down by exterior, interior, engine compartment, storage compartment (trunk), and undercarriage. Groups of judges scrutinize every car and give points for each section of the automobile they judge. Points can be taken away for dirt and imperfections.

When all the points are added up, an award is given for the best in each division. Then these first-placed winners are rejudged to determine the Best of Show.

Receiving the highest award in a national show can add to the resale value of the automobile.

Most devoted car lovers show their Porsches at least once in the car's life. There are a few event regulars who become obsessed with cleaning and shining every nut and bolt. Why would anyone spend so many hours just for points? There is no complete answer to this question. Some do it to relax, some to see old friends at the events, some even to get out of the house; each person has his or her own reasons.

To find out about events, you should watch the papers or call local car clubs. Events can be local with individual car clubs or a full international collection, such as the Pebble Beach, California, Concours d'Elegance each August on the eighteenth hole of the green overlooking the bay. The cars are entered by invitation only, but the event is open to the casual observer.

pension for thirteen months. Any car involved in a crash, or having contact with another car sufficient to produce body, frame, or suspension damage, is automatically withdrawn from the event. (This rule does not apply to all vintage organizations.)

The greatest advantage of this type of racing is that it is usually a family affair. When going to an event to watch, you can bring everyone along, walk around the pit area, and look at the cars being prepared.

At some events there is an extra charge in addition to your entry ticket to get into the paddock area, but it is worth the price. Don't forget your camera. You will see cars that you have never seen before, and some you possibly have never even heard of. You will always see Porsches at these races. Vintage and historic events can give the spectator the feeling of stepping back in time to the late 1950s when these cars were the latest and fastest.

It is easy to find out what track is closest to you. Publications that are helpful to consult are: *Victory Lane*, a monthly magazine based in Palo Alto, California; *Vintage Motorsport*, a bimonthly from Lakeland; Florida; *Grassroots Motorsports*, from Daytona, Florida; *Sports Car World*, from Lindfield, NSW, Australia; *Classic and Sports Car*, from Teddington, England; and *British Car*, from Canoga Park, California.

A few non-Porsche cars you may want to look for around the track are: Scarab, Chaparral, Ford GT, Cobra, Ferrari, Lotus, MG, Birdcage Maserati, Aston-Martin, AMC Javelin, Triumph, Austin-Healey Sprite, and Allard. You might find a Monsterati, Giaur, Peerless LM, Taraschi F-Jr., or Ginetta G4. See you at the races.

CHAPTER EIGHT

A PARTNER IN MOTORING PLEASURE

Page 138: A 1955 Porsche Continental coupe. The "continental" name was used only during this model year, for the United States market only. White wall tires, extremely rare on recent Porsches, were not uncommon on the earlier cars. Page 139: Hood ornament from a 1960-61 Porsche 356B.

THE PORSCHE MYSTIQUE

A true Porsche fanatic fits into the space between the world as it is and the mystical. It is a way of life; it can continue throughout a person's life or only stay with him or her as long as he or she owns the car. It is a wonderful attitude, a point of view, a steadfast faith, and even a warm feeling all over. A true car lover understands this motto, this feeling.

To own a Porsche is an experience whether the car is brand new, direct from the showroom floor, or a previously owned model. There is nothing to compare to owning a sports car like the Porsche. No other marque is engineered like the Porsche. The Weissach engineers call it the leading edge. It has heritage, breeding, and a special elegance.

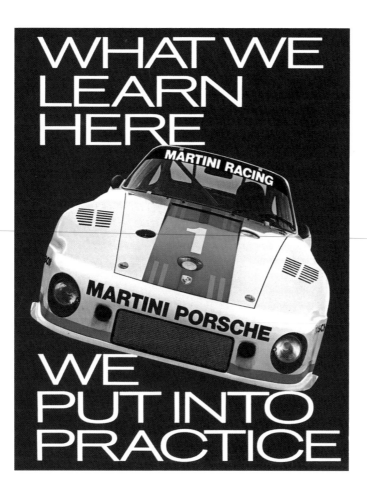

No other automobile company has had a history of as many accomplishments, has advanced the newest technology, won as many races, or continued its dedication to its customers as Porsche has done. First-time Porsche buyers may not even know about any of these factors at the time they are buying their cars. The first-time Porsche buyer may have wanted this automobile since a very young age, may have always talked of owning such a car, and now the time has come to take delivery.

The excitement may be hidden. The feeling may not show for days. But just let someone try to borrow it, and all that hidden apprehension of loss comes flooding through to the new Porsche owner. Of course, it is insured, of course, they will take good care of it, of course! The new Porsche owner would rather lend out the children than lend out the car. And, yes, it does come back in good shape, but that strange feeling of attachment has added to the mystique of owning a Porsche. There is nothing that quite compares to owning a Porsche and in many cases, many Porsches.

PORSCHE CLUBS

After you have taken delivery of your Porsche and have had some time to get acquainted, you may be ready to join a club. There are many advantages of a Porsche club membership, and they start with other Porsche owners. The Porsche Club of America is the largest independent single marque sports car club in the world. It began when a group of Porsche owners held their first meeting in 1955 to exchange ideas on maintaining their cars. They called them "gripe sessions," because it was difficult to get replacement parts and tires to fit correctly in the 1950s. Each owner had his or her own resources, and this was a great way of sharing. Through one of those sessions, for example, one car owner found out that Sears carried

A 1959 GT Speedster.

motorcycle tires that would fit the 356, which were less expensive than ordering from Germany.

By its twenty-fifth anniversary in 1980, the Porsche Club of America had grown into more than 108 regions throughout the continental United States, Alaska, Hawaii, Canada, and Germany. The total membership was over 14,000. Today, there are over 20,000 members in more than 125 regions of the world.

The objectives have stayed the same since that first day. It remains a group that shares friendship, goodwill, and the joy of owning a Porsche. The club provides many benefits for the Porsche owner. (Yes, you do have to own a Porsche and be at least eighteen years old.) One of the most beneficial elements of becoming a member is the monthly magazine, *Porsche Panorama*, containing technical how-to articles, racing news, restoration tips, and the latest new model introductions. There is always information on local and national activities and pages and pages of "For Sale" and "Wanted" sections for cars, parts, and pieces.

The individual local regions across North America have extensive activities including rallies, autocrosses, slaloms, gymkhanas, concours d'elegance, time trials, driver's schools, autocross schools, rally schools, dinner meetings, cocktail parties, picnics, banquets, technical sessions, work sessions, tune-up sessions, and general entertainment. Each local region also has its own newsletter for local members.

Once a year the PCA stages its Porsche Parade. This week-long convention of Porsche enthusiasts is held each year in a different location, usually during the warm weather. Members come from all over the country and abroad. It is hosted by a volunteering region, and members participate in a range of activities, from driving events and technical activities to a full point concours d'elegance and a rally. Trophies are earned for individual events and door prizes are awarded each day. Porsche factory officials come to the parade to conduct seminars. Often the factory delegation includes a member of the Porsche family.

When it is all added up, it is really a wonderful idea. A Porsche owner can just pick out what to be involved with and enjoy the ride.

There are more than 300 Porsche clubs in 33 countries, totaling more than 125,000 members.

Porsche Club of America, P.O. Box 30100, Alexandria, VA 22310, USA.18

Porsche Club of South Australia, P.O. Box 43, Glen Osmond, SA 5064, Australia.

Porsche Club Belgique, Steenweg op Leuven 639, B-3071 Kortengerg, Belgium.

Porsche Club Deutschland, Adolf Kronerstrasse 18, D-70184 Stuttgart, Germany.

Porsche Club Espana, Paseo de la Castellana 62, Madrid 28046, Spain.

Porsche Club de France, c/o Texport SA, 29-31 Rue d'Alger BP646, 76007 Rouen, France.

Porsche Club Great Britain, Ayton House, West End, Northleach, Cheltenham, Gloucestershire GL54 3HG, England.

Porsche Club of Holland, Papehof 39, NL 1391 BE, Abcoude, Netherlands.

Porsche Club Hong Kong, 227 Prince Edward Road, 1/F Block A, Kowloon, Hong Kong.

Porsche Club Italia, Via Guerrazzi 22, 20145, Milano, Italy.

Porsche Owners Club of Japan, 16-21 Meguro-Honcho 2-Chome Meguro-ku, Tokyo, 152 Japan.
Nederlandse Porsche Club, Huisdreef 1, NL 4851 RA, Ulvenhout, Netherlands.

Porsche Club of New South Wales, P.O. Box 183, Lindfield, NSW 2070, Australia.

Porsche Club New Zealand, P.O. Box 33-1074, Auckland 9, New Zealand.

Porsche Klubb Norge, Postboks 83 Lilleaker, N-0216 Oslo, Norway.

Porsche Club South Africa, P.O. Box 72102, Parkview, 2122 South Africa.

Porsche Club Sverige, P.O. Box 34025, S-10026, Stockholm, Sweden.

Porsche Club of Victoria, P.O. Box 911, Kew, Victoria 3101, Australia.

Porsche Club of Western Australia, P.O. Box 447, South Perth, Western Australia 6151.

356 Registry

Another club that is relatively small, with about 5,000 members, is the 356 Registry, whose primary interest centers on the early Porsches. The club's low-key weekends are designed around swap meets, concours, touring, and banquets. The club has a high participation level, with events called "Holidays," topped off by a swap meet. Venders can sell Porsche "stuff," but the best part is finding the missing piece of your car that you have needed for ten years.

For more information contact:
Barbara Skirmants
356 Registry, 27244 Ryan Road, Warren, MI 28092

19TH PORSCHE PARADE POCONO '74

30 YEARS PORSCHE PARADE 1985
COSTA MESA - CALIFORNIA
PCA - ZONE 8

PORSCHE PARADE 24
FOUNDING REGION POTOMAC
SILVER ANNIVERSARY 25 YEARS PCA

1981 WEST COAST HOLIDAY V 356 REGISTRY

Aspen '78 COLORADO
TWENTY-THIRD PORSCHE PARADE

PORSCHE

17th PORSCHE PARADE CHICAGO REGION PCA

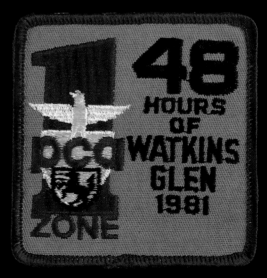

48 HOURS OF WATKINS GLEN 1981
PCA ZONE

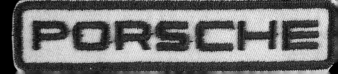

PORSCHE

CHAPTER NINE

AUTOMOTIVE ART AND THE PORSCHE

What is automotive art? It is easy to state what it is *not*: automotive art is not the art of painting a flame job on the side of your Porsche! Automotive art is the image and form of the car, whether it be a racing scene or just the scaled-down automobile standing alone. The art piece can take many forms, from a sculpture in ceramic or wood to a painting in oils or watercolors to a serigraph. There are many types of automotive art today, available through special showings, advertisements in automotive magazines and newspapers, trackside art shows, or direct purchase from artists or dealers.

The earliest automotive art goes back to pre–World War I, when speed and mobility were associated with the excitement of the new motorcar. The art took the form of posters, commercial prints, stained glass, and even fine art including crystal figurines depicting the automobile. The medium had no boundaries; it sold to the automotive admirer.

Automotive artists include names we are very familiar with. Henri Toulouse-Lautrec (1864–1901) sketched the earliest automobiles, and after the war, the French artist F. Gordon Crosby (1885–1942) painted racing scenes from Le Mans. René Lalique's (1860–1945) first automotive work was in bronze and enamels, and later in glass. He became famous in Paris as a goldsmith and jeweller. Today, Lalique's original signed molded glass pieces of animals and women from radiator hood ornaments (car mascots) are very sought-after items. Even Henry Matisse (1869–1954) painted *La Route de Villacoublay* in 1917, a scene from the perspective of the backseat of a right-hand drive automobile.

Another artist who depicted the automobile was Ernest Montaut (1879–1909), whose technique gave his images a dramatic sense of speed. Other artists, such as René Vincent (1879–1936) and Geo Ham (Georges Hamel, 1900–1972) specialized in poster art. Many of their designs were used as illustrations for magazines and newspapers. Much of the time the drawings took the form of caricatures because of the amusing adventures that occurred during the early days of the motorcar.

In the 1920s and 1930s, much of the automotive art was seen in Europe, where sports racing was quite common. If there was a race going on, there were always artists sketching scenes to re-create the historical incident. Many of the poster pieces were used to advertise a specific event such as an exposition of the horseless carriage or an automobile club event. Of course, at that time none of this work was called fine art. None of it was shown in galleries or even hung in private homes as wall art. Most of these designs, sketches, or illustrations were, sadly, thrown away after the event or after being used to illustrate a newspaper article.

Also at this time, the art of decorating watch cases and penknives with a motoring theme became fashionable. Some of the early collectible pieces that have lasted over time started as awards that were given out for a particular racing event. These awards were made in bronze and sometimes ceramic, depicting a popular entry of the race. The art of collecting anything that has to do with the automobile can go on forever.

Many artists, such as Norman Rockwell (1894–1978) and Maxfield Parrish (1870–1966), did not specialize in the automobile but used the car frequently in their work. And as the motorcar became a household word, the automobile manufacturers used the art to sell their products. It was easy to stylize or exaggerate a painting of the latest automobile even before the product was manufactured. Even into the 1950s, Porsche sales literature used illustrations of the next year's models rather than photographs. By the time the cars were delivered, they did not always look much like the picture in the brochure. Finding these early sales brochures is a collectible art form by itself.

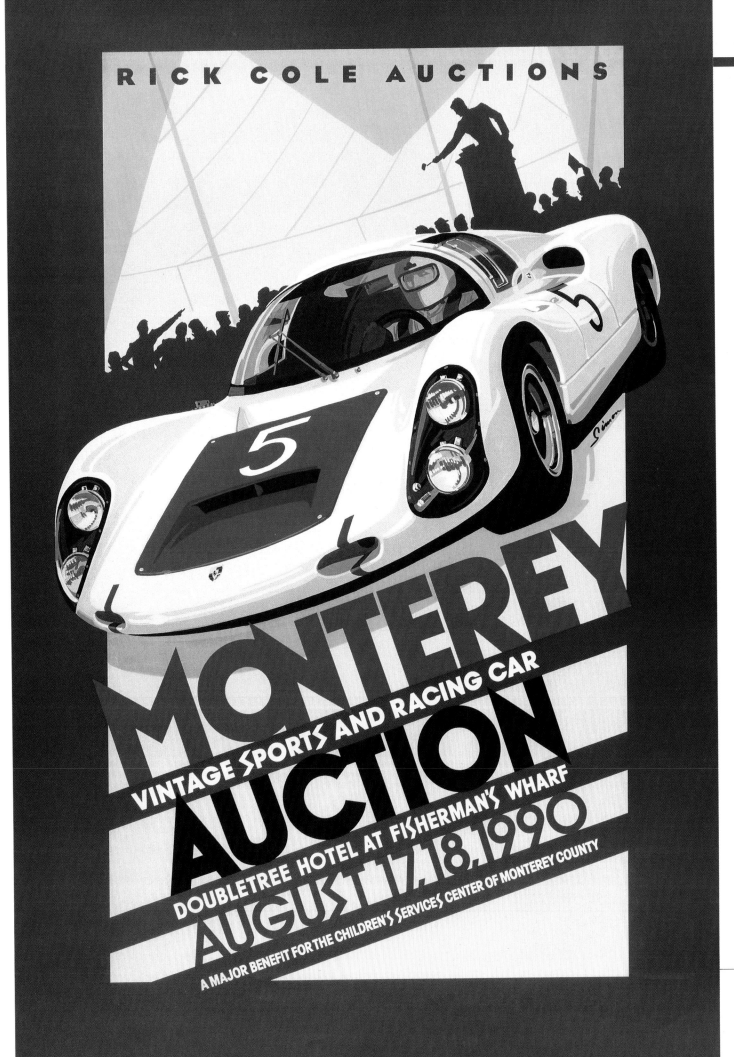

Dennis Simon creates stylized images of classic sports and racing cars in his poster art. This image of a Porsche Carrera 6 was created for the Rick Cole Auction in Monterey, California, in 1990.

Below: Glöckler–Porsche at
Montlhery 1951, *Edition 21,*
by Lawrence A. Braun.
The stainless steel sculpture
on black lacquered hard-
wood celebrates the record-
breaking endurance race
in September 1951.
Opposite page, left: Porsche
Invitational '91, *a piece of*
poster art by Dennis Simon,
is a collage of Porsche cars
and their drivers. **Opposite**
page, right: Four-Cam
Mechanic by Lawrence A.
Braun, *with a polished*
stainless steel engine, and
bronze figure and stand.

Since World War II, most of the automotive art has been shown for sale in the United States; many European artists have chosen to show their art in North America. The shows can be public or private, and if the work is racing-oriented, it is often seen at racetracks across the country. The latest hot market has turned out to be Japan. Many Japanese collectors are car lovers, who do not have the available garage space to own multiple vehicles; it is much easier for them to buy many pieces of automotive art.

Today, automotive fine art can also be seen for sale at famous auction houses before actual rare automobiles are brought up before the auction block. It is very difficult to estimate prices of new and old art; like other types of art, the price depends on the buyer at the moment of sale. An automotive enthusiast is well advised to buy what he or she likes, and not what he or she thinks may

appreciate in the next few years. Hang it in the garage, in the den, in the bedroom, even in the kitchen, but make sure to enjoy your investment.

Many kinds of automotive art are available to collect. Selective artists' works have been appreciating each year, and now that automotive art has been accepted by the public as "art," your likes and dislikes are the only thing that will hold you back. If you are on a limited budget, a poster can be acquired for a small amount of money; getting the artist to sign the poster will increase its value. If the poster is racing-oriented, another way to add to the value is to find the driver of the car that is shown in the poster or even the owner of the car and ask for his or her autograph.

For a little more money, one can acquire a limited edition poster or a lithograph that is signed and numbered. Sometimes the subject is an event; other times it can be

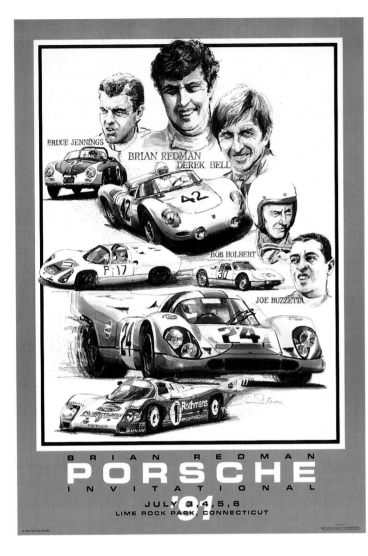

a specific race or a specific automobile. The price range depends on the number printed and signed and the reputation of the artist.

After poster art, the range of work is unlimited. There are artists who specialize in bronze sculptures, such as Lawrence A. Braun, who casts in a very limited number by the lost-wax process. Braun's subjects can be the bust of a famous driver, an automobile creator, or a special car winning a race. Another artist who works in bronze is Stanley Wanlass, who often adds a hand-painted patina to his subject or presents his work in sterling silver. Wanlass often selects his models from his own collection of restored automobiles.

Top: *This signed lithograph by Nicholas A. Watts is titled Paris–Dakar Rally 1986. Bottom: This limited edition serigraph signed by the artist Randy Owens is titled Holbert/Bell/962. Opposite page: James Dean in his 550 Spyder by Stanley Wanlass. This limited edition sculpture was available in bronze, sterling silver, and hand-painted patina on bronze (shown here). Wanlass captures the automobile in motion.*

Another style of sculpture is created by Robert Hossack, who uses the Raku firing process, which creates a crackle finish with carbon highlights. Each sculpture of a classic or exotic automobile is unique in design and sometimes slightly exaggerated to create character in each of the pieces.

Another talented artist is Randy Owens, who is a master silkscreen printmaker. His original impressions (also called serigraphs) are very colorful and limited in edition size to about one hundred copies. Owens almost exclusively uses the race car as his subject. His images are also signed by the race drivers who have driven those machines.

The art of painting in gouache on paper has been perfected by the German artist Walter Gotschke. His work is deceptively impressionistic; the subject matter ranges from hill-climb racing of the 1950s through the cars of the 1990s, with each scene telling a story.

Another artist living in Germany is Carlo Demand, whose automobile art can be seen in six books that he has illustrated. The latest, *Porsche Renngeschichte In Bildern*, is all Porsche-related.

A few other names of artists who work you can look for when auto art collecting are: Jesse Alexander, Harold Cleworth, Ken Dallison, Ken Eberts, Dave Friedman, Jerry Gambacinni, Peter Helck, Andreas Hentrich, Jack Juratovic, Jay Koka, Phyllis Krim, Sandra Leitzinger, David Lord, William Motta, Bill Neale, J. Paul Nesse, Charles Queener, Dennis Simon, Bill Stahl, Erich Strenger, and Michael Turner. There are also many more artists who are well known and greatly admired, such as Leo Bestgen, Paul Bracq, Melbourne Brindle, Dennis Brown, John Burgess, Sr., Dennis Fritz, Tom Hale, Dennis Hoyt,

Nicholas Watts, Nicola Wood, and Emanuel Zurini, in addition to many others.

The artists mentioned who are still selling their original works are relatively affordable. There is always a starting point—visit a gallery, go to a race, or even talk to the artist about his or her work. Some of these artists have illustrated books or may have books published about their art forms. There are lots of ways to collect. Even pages from old *Saturday Evening Post* magazines that are in frameable condition are sold at flea markets.

There are a few excellent galleries specializing in automotive items including original art, such as l'art et l'automobile in New York City. On the West Coast of the United States there is Crossroads Motoring Gallery in Carmel, California. In Canada you can visit Gallery Five Hundred Ltd. in Ontario; in British Columbia, there is Bob & Wally's Gallery of Automotive Art. One particularly interesting gallery, called Le Garage, is located in Tokyo and Kobe, Japan.

The exclusive Automotive Fine Arts Society produces a publication specializing in automotive art titled *AFAS (Automotive Fine Arts Society) Quarterly*. To inquire about a subscription, contact: GP/Publishing Inc., P.O. Box 325, Lake Orion, MI 48361-0325. The magazine features members as well as independent artists, and the organization sponsors one show a year in Pebble Beach, California, during the famous Concours d'Elegance in August. Many of the artists are in attendance, so you have the opportunity to ask questions and talk with them about their creations. During the same weekend there is also the Laguna Seca Historic Race, where you get the opportunity to see the early cars that the artists have used in their works of art. You can also see displays by individual artists at many of the CART and Formula 1 races from the the Meadowlands in New Jersey to Adelaide, Australia. So enjoy hunting for that treasured piece of art celebrating the joy of car watching.

Coca-Cola serigraph by Randy Owens. Available in a limited issue of ninety-five prints, with forty signed by the drivers Bob Akin, Hans Stuck, and Jo Gartner.

APPENDIX

Galleries Specializing in Automotive Art and Other Motoring Goodies

Art and Automobile Ltd, Regalo 4-4 Natsugi-Cho, Nishinomiya 662, Japan

Bob & Wally's Gallery of Automotive Art, 570 Clark Drive, Vancouver, British Columbia, Canada V5L 3H6

Car's The Star, 2450 Grand Avenue, Crown Center #202, Kansas City, MO 64108

Car's The Star, LaPlaza Mall, 2200 South 10th, McAllen, TX 78503

Galerie Vitesse, 48 Rue de Berri, 75008 Paris, France

Gallery Automania, 304 East Street, Rochester, MI 48307

Khachadourian Gallery, 60 Pall Mall, London, SW1 Y5HZ England

l'art el l'automobile, 121 Madison Avenue, New York, NY 10016

Le Garage, 5-17-1 Roppongi Minato-ku, Tokyo, 106, Japan

Le Garage, 4-1-14, Kaigandori, Chuo-ku, Kobe, 650, Japan

The Motorsport Collector, 5120 Bellmont Road, Suite S, Downers Grove, IL 60515

Crossroads Motoring Gallery, 169 Crossroads Boulevard, Carmel, CA 93923

The Scuderia, 1721 Lakeshore Road West, Mississauga, Ontario, Canada L5J 1J4

Wine Country Motor Sports, 28001 Arnold Drive, Sonoma, CA 95476

Many of the above locations include memorabilia such as mascots, books, posters, miniatures, sales literature, and inscribed photographs as well as original art.

BIBLIOGRAPHY

Batchelor, Dean. *Illustrated Porsche Buyers Guide*. Osceola, Wisc.: Motorbooks International, 1982.

Clarke, R. M. comp. *Porsche 914, 1969-1983*. Cobham, Surrey, England: Reprint division, Brookland Book Distribution, Ltd., 1985.

——. *Porsche 924, 1975-1981*. Cobham, Surrey, England: Reprint division, Brookland Book Distribution, Ltd., 1982.

Cotton, Michael. *Porsche 924 and 944*. Huddersfield, West Yorkshire, England: The Amadeus Press Ltd., 1990.

Fujimoto, Akira, and Giancarlo Perini. *Porsche & Design, Car Styling Vol. 31 1/2*. Tokyo, Japan: San'ei Shobo Publishing, Co., Ltd., 1980.

Georgano, G. N., ed. *The Complete Encyclopedia of Motorcars*. New York: E. P. Dutton & Co., 1970.

——. *The Complete Encyclopedia of Motor Sport*. New York: Viking Press, Inc., 1971.

Grun, Bernard. *The Timetables of History*. New York: Simon and Schuster, 1979.

Harvey, Chris. *Great Marques: Porsche*. London, England: Octopus Books, Ltd., 1980.

Hindsdale, Peter. *The Fabulous Porsche 917*. South Laguna, Calif.: Jonathan Thompson Publishing, 1972.

Jenkinson, Dennis. *Porsche 356*. London, England: Osprey Publishing Ltd., 1980.

Kimes, Beverly Rae. *The Star and the Laurel*. Montvale, N.J.: Mercedes-Benz of North America, 1986.

Lewis, Lucinda. *Porsche: The Fine Art of the Sports Car*. San Diego: Thunder Bay Press, 1990.

Ludvigsen, Karl. *Porsche: Excellence Was Expected*. Princeton, N.J.: Princeton Publishing, Inc., 1977.

McCarthy, Jim. *Vintage Racing!! Start to Finish*. Sparta, Wisc.: RPM Enterprises Ltd., 1990.

Miller, Susann C. *Porsche 911, A Source Book 1974-84*. Baltimore: Bookman Publishing, 1985.

——. *Porsche 911/912, A Source Book 1963-73*. Baltimore: Bookman Publishing, 1984.

——. *Porsche Year 1982*. Laurel Hollow, N.Y.: Carrera International, Inc., 1982.

——. *Porsche Year 1983-84*. Clifton, Va.: M&M Publishing, 1984.

——. *Porsche Year 1985-86*. Clifton, Va.: M&M Publishing, 1986.

Miller, Susann C., and Richard F. Merritt. *Porsche: Brochures and Sales Literature, A Source Book, 1948-1965*. Clifton, Va.: M&M Publishing, 1985.

Morgan, Peter. *Original Porsche 911*. Devon, England: Bay View Books, Ltd., 1995.

Porsche, Dr. Ing. h.c. Ferry, and Gunther Molter. *Ferry Porsche: Cars Are My Life*. Northamptonshire, England: Patrick Stephens Ltd., 1989.

Sloniger, Jerry. *Porsche 924-944-928: The New Generation*. London, England: Osprey Publishing Ltd., 1981.

——. *Porsche, the 4-Cylinder, 4-Cam Sports & Racing Cars*. Reno, Nev.: db publications, 1977.

Strache, Dr. Wolfe, comp. *100 Years of Porsche Mirrored in Contemporary History*. Stuttgart, Germany: Dr. Ing. h.c.F. Porsche AG, 1975.

Tubbs, D. B. *Art and the Automobile*. New York: Grosset & Dunlap, 1978.

Upietz, Ulrich. *Porsche Sport '93*. Duisburg, Germany: Gruppe C Motorsport-Verlag GmbH, 1993.

——. *Porsche Sport '94*. Duisburg, Germany: Gruppe C Motorsport-Verlag GmbH, 1994.

Weitmann, Julius, and Rico Steinemann. *Project 928*. Stuttgart, Germany: Motorbuch Verlag, 1977.

PHOTOGRAPHY CREDITS:

INDEX